T0194666

An Analysis of

Daniel Jonah Goldhagen's

Hitler's Willing Executioners

Simon Taylor
with
Tom Stammers

Published by Macat International Ltd
24:13 Coda Centre, 189 Munster Road, London SW6 6AW.

Distributed exclusively by Routledge
2 Park Square, Milton Park, Abingdon, Oxon OX14 4RN
711 Third Avenue, New York, NY 10017, USA

Routledge is an imprint of the Taylor & Francis Group, an informa business

www.macat.com
info@macat.com

Cataloguing in Publication Data
A catalogue record for this book is available from the British Library.
Library of Congress Cataloguing-in-Publication Data is available upon request.
Cover illustration: Etienne Gilfillan

ISBN 978-1-912302-60-4 (hardback)
ISBN 978-1-912128-41-9 (paperback)
ISBN 978-1-912281-48-0 (e-book)

Notice

CONTENTS

WAYS IN TO THE TEXT

Who Is Daniel Jonah Goldhagen?   9

What Does *Hitler's Willing Executioners* Say?   10

Why Does *Hitler's Willing Executioners* Matter?   12

SECTION 1: INFLUENCES

Module 1: The Author and the Historical Context   15

Module 2: Academic Context   19

Module 3: The Problem   23

Module 4: The Author's Contribution   27

SECTION 2: IDEAS

Module 5: Main Ideas   33

Module 6: Secondary Ideas   38

Module 7: Achievement   43

Module 8: Place in the Author's Work   48

SECTION 3: IMPACT

Module 9: The First Responses   54

Module 10: The Evolving Debate   59

Module 11: Impact and Influence Today   64

Module 12: Where Next?   69

Glossary of Terms   75

People Mentioned in the Text   83

Works Cited   90

THE MACAT LIBRARY

The Macat Library is a series of unique academic explorations of seminal works in the humanities and social sciences – books and papers that have had a significant and widely recognised impact on their disciplines. It has been created to serve as much more than just a summary of what lies between the covers of a great book. It illuminates and explores the influences on, ideas of, and impact of that book. Our goal is to offer a learning resource that encourages critical thinking and fosters a better, deeper understanding of important ideas.

Each publication is divided into three Sections: Influences, Ideas, and Impact. Each Section has four Modules. These explore every important facet of the work, and the responses to it.

This Section-Module structure makes a Macat Library book easy to use, but it has another important feature. Because each Macat book is written to the same format, it is possible (and encouraged!) to cross-reference multiple Macat books along the same lines of inquiry or research. This allows the reader to open up interesting interdisciplinary pathways.

To further aid your reading, lists of glossary terms and people mentioned are included at the end of this book (these are indicated by an asterisk [*] throughout) – as well as a list of works cited.

Macat has worked with the University of Cambridge to identify the elements of critical thinking and understand the ways in which six different skills combine to enable effective thinking.
Three allow us to fully understand a problem; three more give us the tools to solve it. Together, these six skills make up the **PACIER** model of critical thinking. They are:

ANALYSIS – understanding how an argument is built
EVALUATION – exploring the strengths and weaknesses of an argument
INTERPRETATION – understanding issues of meaning

CREATIVE THINKING – coming up with new ideas and fresh connections
PROBLEM-SOLVING – producing strong solutions
REASONING – creating strong arguments

To find out more, visit **WWW.MACAT.COM.**

CRITICAL THINKING AND *HITLER'S WILLING EXECUTIONERS*

Primary critical thinking skill: EVALUATION
Secondary critical thinking skill: INTERPRETATION

Daniel Goldhagen's study of the Holocaust offers conclusions that run directly counter to those reached by Christopher Browning, whose book *Ordinary Men* is also the subject of a Macat analysis. As such, the two analyses make possible some interesting critical thinking exercises focused on evaluation of the evidence used by the two historians. For Goldhagen, a chief reason for German actions was not the mundane good comradeship stressed by Browning, but a longstanding hatred of Jews and Judaism specific to Germany that dated back well into the previous century. Debating which historian is right, which has made better use of the available evidence, which has most successfully written objectively – and which advances the most secure interpretation of contested documents – forces students to think critically about one of the most important and (on the surface at least) incomprehensible events of the past century.

ABOUT THE AUTHOR OF THE ORIGINAL WORK

The son of a Holocaust survivor, American writer **Daniel Jonah Goldhagen** was born in 1959. After gaining his doctorate from Harvard University in 1992, Goldhagen was employed as an assistant professor in the department of Government and Social Studies there. His 1996 book *Hitler's Willing Executioners* gained a wide readership and became a global bestseller, but it created academic controversy, with most scholars fiercely criticizing Goldhagen's ideas about the Holocaust. Following the publication of his second book, *A Moral Reckoning*, in 2002 Goldhagen resigned from his academic post to take up writing full time.

ABOUT THE AUTHORS OF THE ANALYSIS

Dr Simon Taylor holds PhD in modern history from Columbia University. He is currently undertaking postdoctoral research at the University of Chicago.

Dr Thomas Stammers is lecturer in Modern European history at Durham University, where he specialises in the cultural history of France in the age of revolution. He is the author of *Collection, Recollection, Revolution: Scavenging the Past in Nineteenth-Century Paris*. Dr Stammers's research interests include a wide range of historiographical and theoretical controversies related to eighteenth and nineteenth-century Europe.

ABOUT MACAT

GREAT WORKS FOR CRITICAL THINKING

Macat is focused on making the ideas of the world's great thinkers accessible and comprehensible to everybody, everywhere, in ways that promote the development of enhanced critical thinking skills.

It works with leading academics from the world's top universities to produce new analyses that focus on the ideas and the impact of the most influential works ever written across a wide variety of academic disciplines. Each of the works that sit at the heart of its growing library is an enduring example of great thinking. But by setting them in context – and looking at the influences that shaped their authors, as well as the responses they provoked – Macat encourages readers to look at these classics and game-changers with fresh eyes. Readers learn to think, engage and challenge their ideas, rather than simply accepting them.

'Macat offers an amazing first-of-its-kind tool for interdisciplinary learning and research. Its focus on works that transformed their disciplines and its rigorous approach, drawing on the world's leading experts and educational institutions, opens up a world-class education to anyone.'

Andreas Schleicher
Director for Education and Skills, Organisation for Economic Co-operation and Development

'Macat is taking on some of the major challenges in university education ... They have drawn together a strong team of active academics who are producing teaching materials that are novel in the breadth of their approach.'

Prof Lord Broers,
former Vice-Chancellor of the University of Cambridge

'The Macat vision is exceptionally exciting. It focuses upon new modes of learning which analyse and explain seminal texts which have profoundly influenced world thinking and so social and economic development. It promotes the kind of critical thinking which is essential for any society and economy.
This is the learning of the future.'

Rt Hon Charles Clarke, former UK Secretary of State for Education

'The Macat analyses provide immediate access to the critical conversation surrounding the books that have shaped their respective discipline, which will make them an invaluable resource to all of those, students and teachers, working in the field.'

Professor William Tronzo, University of California at San Diego

WAYS IN TO THE TEXT

KEY POINTS

- Daniel Jonah Goldhagen was an American historian who taught at Harvard before giving up his post to concentrate on writing for a wider audience.

- *Hitler's Willing Executioners* argues that the German people actively endorsed the genocidal* policies of the Nazis*—the party that ruled Germany under Adolf Hitler* from 1933 to 1945.

- The book is distinctive for claiming the Holocaust*—the systematic murder of roughly six million Jews*—happened because there was popular hatred of the Jews. Goldhagen calls this "eliminationist* anti-Semitism."*

Who Is Daniel Jonah Goldhagen?

The American historian Daniel Jonah Goldhagen was born in Boston in 1959. In 1996, at the age of just 37, he published *Hitler's Willing Executioners: Ordinary Germans and the Holocaust*, a book based on a doctoral dissertation he had written at Harvard University. It immediately brought him both celebrity and notoriety. Why? Because in the book Goldhagen argues that it was the German nation as a whole that was responsible for the mass killing of European Jews in the 1940s. Genocide*—the systematic destruction of a racial, religious, or ethnic group—happened simply because the German people wanted it to happen.

Goldhagen's father, Erich Goldhagen, had himself survived the Holocaust. After World War II* he left Europe for America and became a history professor at Harvard, specializing in the study of Nazi crimes, particularly against the Jews. Erich's experiences and work clearly inspired his son; Daniel also went on to study the people who had allowed the Holocaust to happen.

After gaining his doctorate at Harvard, Daniel took a job at the university, becoming an assistant professor in the Department of Government and Social Studies. Four years later he published his first book, *Hitler's Willing Executioners*. Consciously aimed at both academics and the wider reading public, it immediately divided opinion, with many historians publishing fierce criticism of Goldhagen's sweeping argument. The book was a huge commercial success, though, and soared up the bestseller lists, going on to be translated into 12 languages. It was particularly important in Germany, where Goldhagen became a celebrity commentator.

Six years later, in 2002, Goldhagen published his second book, *A Moral Reckoning*. Again he caused controversy, because this time he accused the Catholic Church of colluding in Nazi crimes against the Jews. A year later Goldhagen gave up his academic position at Harvard to become a full-time writer. His most recent work looks at genocides worldwide.

What Does *Hitler's Willing Executioners* Say?

Many historians have tried to understand exactly why the Holocaust happened. The ideology of Nazi leaders was identified as one reason, while another was that the German conquest of Europe provided the opportunity for large-scale mass murder. But in *Hitler's Willing Executioners* Goldhagen approaches the question in a different way. Instead of looking at the Nazi elite, he focuses on the German population as a whole. What was the mindset of the "ordinary Germans" who had voted Hitler into power in 1933? Why had they complied with Nazi orders and gone along with a policy of mass murder? Goldhagen's central idea is a simple one. German citizens had been willing for the Jews to be murdered because they hated them.

Goldhagen argues that this hatred had been part of the German psyche for centuries and that it had begun as a religious prejudice. Protestant German   states had broken with the Catholic Church back in the sixteenth century. The champion of this new form of Christianity was a monk called Martin Luther,* who was profoundly anti-Jewish; in his sermons he attacked the Jews as the murderers of Christ. In the nineteenth century this anti-Jewish feeling was compounded by new scientific ideas about race. Some theorists and doctors tried to provide biological explanations for the diversity between human cultures, often with the intention of "proving" that one race was superior to another. Racial prejudice against the Jews fed into the old religious prejudice. The result, Goldhagen argues, was a toxic form of anti-Semitism found only in Germany. He called it "eliminationist anti-Semitism," as he believed that the desire to eliminate the Jews from the German nation was at its heart. This could be achieved by a number of means, including converting Jews to Christianity, expelling them from the country or confining them to ghettoes.

In *Hitler's Willing Executioners* Goldhagen says this irrational hatred had grown over the centuries. It had not only carried Adolf Hitler to power in the 1930s, but also led to the failure of the leaders of Germany's churches to speak out when they saw Jews being persecuted. Goldhagen's thesis proposes that German hatred of the Jews was psychotic. He insists that millions of ordinary Germans in the 1930s and 1940s had been fully aware of what was happening to the Jews and that they rejoiced in the killing.

He also rejects the arguments of historians who suggested that the Germans were simply indifferent to the Jews. American historian Christopher Browning* had written a book in 1992 called *Ordinary*

Men. In it he explored why a group of regular Germans (rather than committed Nazis) had obeyed orders to kill thousands of Jews. His conclusion was that they were motivated by fear of authority and a desire to fit in with their peers, rather than a fanatical belief in an ideology. Browning argued that because these were common human motivations, it would be possible for similar atrocities to be carried out by other groups at other times.

Goldhagen dismisses this view. He does not think the Germans were afraid or conformist: he believes they *chose* to act. To illustrate this, he focuses on the ordinary German men and women who worked in the police battalions and labor camps. He also studies those who carried out the death marches.* These marches, which took place after the camps were evacuated in 1944 and 1945, involved moving thousands of prisoners from concentration camps* and prison camps when many were too weak to be moved. Any who could not keep pace were executed. Goldhagen's evidence is drawn from archival research and the testimonies of survivors and witnesses. His conclusion is that there had been widespread eliminationist anti-Semitism in Germany.

Why Does *Hitler's Willing Executioners* Matter?

Hitler's Willing Executioners enjoyed enormous popular sales in Europe and America, and it was particularly successful in Germany. This is one of the reasons Goldhagen's book is important, because it became part of the way in which modern Germany confronted its Nazi past.

But the book also matters because of the enormous controversy it stirred up. In the 1980s, German academics had disagreed about how the Holocaust should be studied. This "historians' quarrel"—or *Historikerstreit**—debated how far the crimes of the Nazis should be compared with the crimes of the Soviet Union,* another brutal regime. Meanwhile, others disputed how far historians should go to try to see events through the eyes of the Nazis themselves.

A decade later, Goldhagen also wanted to consider the views and feelings of the people who had carried out the Holocaust. He believed that to do this it was vital to recognize that their beliefs were radically different from those of the modern world. He insists that the Germans of the early twentieth century were ill. They were suffering from an irrational mental sickness, and this took the form of a warped fantasy about the Jews that they tried to impose on the whole of Europe.

The extremity of Goldhagen's argument attracted readers. It had a seductive appeal for many journalists and ordinary members of the public, and so the book received a huge amount of attention. As a result, historians felt compelled to debunk Goldhagen's conclusions. Scholars accused him of getting his facts wrong and distorting the evidence. They rejected his central idea: that the Germans as a whole displayed a unique form of anti-Semitism. They even accused him of being racist against Germans.

The debate helped historians to reach a consensus about how to approach the study of the Holocaust. At the very least, it focused attention away from the actions of the Nazi elite and toward the behavior of everyday Germans. The scale of the row that Goldhagen generated, both in academic circles and among the general public, revealed the ongoing sensitivity surrounding these issues. But it also showed that there was a huge appetite for writings about this most delicate of historical topics. And Goldhagen also revealed a difficult truth. His ideas, rejected by professional historians, resonated with Holocaust survivors. This forced historians to explain an uncomfortable issue: the possibility that individual experience does not always reveal the full historical truth.

By academic standards, Goldhagen had not written a compelling history. But he did launch a compelling debate.

SECTION 1
INFLUENCES

MODULE 1
THE AUTHOR AND THE HISTORICAL CONTEXT

KEY POINTS

- *Hitler's Willing Executioners* argues—controversially—that ordinary Germans were responsible for the Holocaust.*

- Goldhagen was highly influenced by his father, a Holocaust survivor who became a Harvard historian.

- The Holocaust was subject to a host of new commemorations, representations, and controversies in the 1990s.

Why Read This Text?

Daniel Jonah Goldhagen published *Hitler's Willing Executioners: Ordinary Germans and the Holocaust* in 1996, and it quickly became an international phenomenon. Within a year, it had been translated into 12 languages and had become a best seller in the United States, Britain, and Germany. But Goldhagen's provocative central thesis caused huge controversy. He argues that:

- Ordinary Germans had a deep-seated and violent hatred of Jews*—what he called eliminationist* anti-Semitism.*

- This anti-Semitism had been present in Germany for centuries and was a key part of the national culture.

- Under the Third Reich,* between 1933 and 1945, this resulted in ordinary Germans eagerly and knowingly participating in the Holocaust, the genocide* against the Jews.

- It was not just the Nazis* who were guilty of the Holocaust, but the whole German nation.

> 66 German anti-Semitic beliefs about Jews were
> the central causal agent of the Holocaust ... The
> conclusion of this book is that anti-Semitism moved
> many thousands of 'ordinary' Germans—and
> would have moved millions more, had they been
> appropriately positioned—to slaughter Jews. Not
> economic hardship, not the coercive means of a
> totalitarian state, not the social psychological, not
> invariable psychological propensities, but ideas about
> Jews that were pervasive in Germany, and had been for
> decades, induced ordinary Germans to kill unarmed,
> defenseless Jewish men, women and children by the
> thousands, systematically and without pity... 99
>
> Daniel Jonah Goldhagen, *Hitler's Willing Executioners*

Other historians had previously tried to explain why there had been mass murder of European Jews in the 1930s and 1940s. While some argued that the killing was an unforeseen consequence of World War II,* others suggested that structural factors were to blame, such as internal competition between members of the Nazi leadership. Goldhagen was not moved by these arguments, insisting that many ordinary Germans had willingly participated in the murder. This controversial view drew both praise and severe criticism. The book won a popular audience, but the academic reaction was emphatically negative. Many scholars rejected Goldhagen's views, but the controversy and debate around this huge core idea meant that interest in the book soared. The "Goldhagen Controversy" was one of the major scholarly events of the 1990s and catapulted the author to international fame.

Author's Life

Goldhagen was born in 1959, in Boston, Massachusetts. When he was a child, his father, Erich Goldhagen, briefly moved the family to

Germany. Erich was a Harvard historian and was carrying out research on the Holocaust. After the family's return to America, Daniel won a place at Harvard himself. He did his undergraduate and his doctoral studies there, submitting his doctoral dissertation in 1992. In the same year he was appointed an assistant professor in Harvard's Department of Government and Social Studies. Goldhagen started looking into the possibilities of writing a book based on his dissertation. After making significant revisions, most of which were designed to help the text reach a popular as well as a scholarly audience, he published *Hitler's Willing Executioners* in 1996.

Goldhagen dedicated *Hitler's Willing Executioners* to his father. This was not particularly surprising. As a child, Erich Goldhagen had been interned in the Romanian-Jewish ghetto in Czernowitz (now part of the Ukraine). After leaving Europe for America, he became professor of history and divinity at Harvard University, where he taught a class on the Holocaust for 25 years. In 1971, Erich published a work that exposed Hitler's minister of armaments, Albert Speer.*[1] At the end of World War II,* senior Nazis had been put on trial for their actions. At the Nuremberg Trials,* Speer argued that he knew nothing about the Holocaust. He was sentenced to 20 years in prison for using forced labor, but was deemed not guilty of mass murder. The verdict made Speer the highest-ranking Nazi official to escape execution for his crimes. But Erich Goldhagen argued that Speer *was* aware of the Holocaust. His work looked to demonstrate Speer's complicity in the extermination of the Jews. Like his father, Daniel Jonah Goldhagen would focus on German complicity in the Holocaust.

Author's Background
The Holocaust was a subject of intense debate in the 1990s, both within academia and more widely. As the generation of survivors gradually passed away over the course of the decade, a series of new memorials were built, special installations in museums were created,

and oral testimonies were collected. Landmark films, like the Oscar-winning *Schindler's List* of 1993, heightened awareness of the Holocaust, particularly in America.[2] In 1996, January 27 was decreed a special day of remembrance in Germany. Britain followed in 2001 and the United Nations in 2005. It became a crime in many European countries to deny that the Holocaust had occurred. This wave of commemoration and discussion ensured that there would be an appreciative audience for Goldhagen's provocative book.

During the 1990s there were also controversies over the way the memory of the Holocaust might be manipulated. In the late 1990s, for example, the British historian Richard Evans* was asked to examine the work of another British historian, who stood accused of Holocaust denial.*[3] Even more contentious were allegations that the American media had deliberately invoked the horrors of Jewish suffering to justify the political policies of Israel, with whom America had friendly relations. In the words of the American political scientist Norman Finkelstein,* the Holocaust had become an "industry."[4] These were highly charged debates, which showed that writing about the Holocaust had very real political implications in the present day.

NOTES

1   Erich Goldhagen, "Albert Speer, Himmler and the Secrecy of the Final Solution," *Midstream* (October 1971): 43–50.

2   David Cesarini, "The Aftermath of the Holocaust," *Encyclopedia of the Holocaust*, ed. Shmuel Spector and Robert Rozett (New York and London: Routledge, 2013), 85–100.

3   Richard Evans, *Telling Lies about Hitler: Holocaust, History and the David Irving Trial* (London: Verso, 2002).

4   Norman Finkelstein, *The Holocaust Industry: Reflections on the Exploitation of Jewish Suffering* (London: Verso, 2000).

MODULE 2
ACADEMIC CONTEXT

KEY POINTS

- Historians had debated how the Holocaust* could have happened, and how far the mass killings of Jews* in the 1930s and 1940s could be viewed as the result of previous developments in German and European history.

- Before Goldhagen, historians had explained the Holocaust in terms of "intention" (it happened because people intended it to happen) or "function" (it happened because of the way World War II* unfolded).

- Goldhagen believed he had gone beyond this debate by showing that the urge to eradicate the Jews was the result of deep trends in German culture.

The Work in its Context

Daniel Jonah Goldhagen's book *Hitler's Willing Executioners* was written about one of the greatest tragedies of the twentieth century. The Holocaust demanded—and defied—explanation. Scholars from all disciplines have agreed that the enormity of the suffering involved makes it an almost inexplicable event.[1] In the years immediately after World War II, the annihilation of the Jews was somewhat obscured by the millions of other casualties. But, from the 1960s, the specific nature of the Holocaust became recognized. Yet it remained intensely controversial to compare the targeting and attempted elimination of the Jews with other events. To what degree could it be compared with the murder of other groups, such as those suffering from mental illness? To what degree could it be compared with the killing on the battlefield or with murders in other regimes? In the 1980s German scholarship was rocked by what is known as the *Historikerstreit** or "historians'

f The German perpetrators ... were assenting mass executioners, men and women who, true to their own eliminationist anti-Semitic beliefs, faithful to their cultural anti-Semitic credo, considered the slaughter to be just. 99

Daniel Jonah Goldhagen, *Hitler's Willing Executioners*

quarrel," a fierce spat over whether Nazi* atrocities could be compared with the killings carried out at the same time in the Soviet Union.*

This debate was linked to how far the racial politics of Nazism was seen as a peculiarly German problem. Some historians argued that Germany had developed in a different way from other Western nations. This was called the *Sonderweg** ("special path") thesis. Germany had not become a unified country until 1871, and it had not developed along the same liberal* path as nations such as the United States and Britain. In these countries a political philosophy of liberalism had promoted ideas of individual freedom and moderate, continuous reform. In contrast, the political climate in Germany had allowed authoritarian or racist politics to develop. Two historians particularly associated with a sophisticated form of the *Sonderweg* thesis are the American academics Fritz Stern* and George Mosse.*[2]

Overview of the Field

Before the 1990s, historians of the Holocaust were roughly split into "intentionalists"* and "functionalists."* Functionalists, like the prominent German historian Hans Mommsen,* argued that the Holocaust was neither foreseen nor calculated. They believed that there had never been a coherent plan to exterminate the Jewish people. Instead, the Holocaust was the result of a gradual and unplanned process of radicalization within the Nazi Party leadership. This happened over the course of the war.[3] Mass murder occurred in response to opportunity, such as the conquest of huge swathes of territory in Eastern Europe after 1939. It was also encouraged by the internal dynamics of the Nazi party, as different leaders sought to go further than their rivals. For many functionalists, the decisive event, which changed persecution of the Jews into extermination of the Jews, was the Nazi invasion of the Soviet Union in 1941 and the war that followed. The Nazis believed the Jews were in league with the Communists who ran the Soviet Union. The events of 1941 led to the Jews being seen as an enemy "within" helping the enemy "without" (the Soviet Union).

Intentionalists,* meanwhile, argued that there was a deliberate and premeditated plan by the Nazi hierarchy to carry out the Holocaust.[4] They emphasize the vitriolic hatred expressed in Nazi leader Adolf Hitler's* speeches and in his best-selling memoir, *Mein Kampf.** The cult of personality surrounding Hitler created a heroic, idealized figure. This made it easier for him to impose his views on his followers. Intentionalists also highlight how early the campaign against the Jews began. Hitler became chancellor of Germany in January 1933, and, by that spring, Jewish shops were being boycotted and books by Jewish authors were being burned. This was fully six years before the start of World War II. Intentionalists believe that Hitler demonstrated a consistent desire to destroy the Jewish presence in Germany. His *intentions* explain why he took every opportunity to realize this goal.

Academic Influences

In the late twentieth century the most respected expert on the Holocaust was Saul Friedländer,* a professor of history at the University of California in Los Angeles. Friedländer was born in 1932 into a German-speaking family in Prague, Czechoslovakia, and during World War II his parents died in the gas chambers at Auschwitz.* In 1983, while studying at Harvard University, Goldhagen attended a lecture about the Holocaust given by Friedländer. He later described this as a "lightbulb moment": "Everyone was talking about why the order [to exterminate the Jews] was given, but not about why it was carried out."[5] Friedländer's insight helped Goldhagen to grasp a key issue. To understand the Holocaust, historians shouldn't just ask questions about who gave the orders and when those orders were given. They should ask why so many ordinary citizens went along with those orders.

This is the question that Goldhagen asks in *Hitler's Willing Executioners*, and he believes it was one of the most original and important aspects of the book. His main thesis is that Germans killed Jews during World War II because they were anti-Semitic.* He also argues that there was a uniquely German form of anti-Semitism. This assertion reopened the *Sonderweg** debate: the discussion about whether Germany had somehow developed in a different way from other Western nations. Goldhagen said that the broader public shared his view of German anti-Semitism. He felt that professional historians had chosen to overlook this.[6]

NOTES

1   Saul Friedländer, *Probing the Limits of Representation: Nazism and the Final Solution* (Cambridge MA: Harvard University Press, 1992).

2   See George Mosse, *The Crisis of German Ideology: Intellectual Origins of the Third Reich* (New York: Schocken Books, 1981); Fritz Stern, *The Politics of Cultural Despair: A Study in the Rise of the Germanic Ideology* (Berkeley: University of California Press, 1974).

3   See Hans Mommsen, "Cumulative Radicalisation and Progressive Self-Destruction as Structural Determinants of the Nazi Dictatorship," in *Stalinism and Nazism: Dictatorships in Comparison*, ed. Ian Kershaw and Moshe Lewin (Cambridge: Cambridge University Press, 1997), 75–87.

4   For important examples of the intentionalist position, see Yehuda Bauer, *A History of the Holocaust* (New York: F. Watts, 1982); Eberhard Jäckel and Jürgen Rohwer, eds., *Der Mord an den Juden im Zweiten Weltkrieg: Entschlußbildung und Verwirklichung* (Stuttgart: Deutsche Verlag-Anstalt, 1985).

5   Daniel Jonah Goldhagen, quoted in Dinita Smith, "Challenging a View of the Holocaust," *New York Times*, April 1, 1996.

6   Daniel Jonah Goldhagen, "How Could They Have Done It?," *Harvard University Gazette*, June 6, 1996.

MODULE 3
THE PROBLEM

KEY POINTS

- Goldhagen questions how an event of the magnitude and horror of the Holocaust* occurred, and why so many ordinary Germans had taken part in it.

- American historian Christopher Browning* had studied why ordinary men had murdered Jews* in Germany in the Nazi* era. His view was that peer pressure played a hugely important role.

- Those who put forward the *Sonderweg** thesis alleged that Germany had taken a certain path as a result of toxic German politics. Goldhagen agreed, and believed that most ordinary Germans were driven by culturally deep-set anti-Semitic* hatred.

Core Question

Hitler's Willing Executioners addresses some of the central issues in the wide-ranging debate on the Holocaust:

- Who bore ultimate responsibility for the Holocaust?
- To what extent did ordinary Germans participate in perpetrating the Holocaust?
- Was anti-Semitism in Germany before 1945 in some way different from anti-Semitism in the rest of Europe and the wider world?

These questions had previously been approached by scholars from many disciplines. Some emphasized that the Holocaust was related to impersonal forces, such as the growth of modern bureaucracy and industrial production. These trends reduced the space individuals had

66 The Holocaust was also the defining feature of German politics and political culture during the Nazi period, the most shocking event of the twentieth century, and the most difficult event to understand in all of German history. The Germans' persecution of the Jews culminating in the Holocaust is thus the central feature of Germany during the Nazi period. 99

Daniel Jonah Goldhagen, *Hitler's Willing Executioners*

for moral reflection, and favored efficiency and obedience.[1] Goldhagen, however, presents the Holocaust as a moral drama, emphasizing that it relied on deliberate moral and political choices.

Goldhagen wanted to explore how the policy of exterminating European Jews had come to be carried out. More specifically, he wanted to answer the question as to how and why—from both a moral and a psychological perspective —many thousands of ordinary Germans had participated in what was known by the Nazis as the Final Solution*—the final solution to what they saw as the "Jewish problem." Goldhagen wanted to show that ordinary Germans were willing and eager participants in the Holocaust, and coined the phrase "eliminationist* anti-Semitism"[2] to describe a deep-seated and uniquely German form of hatred toward Jews. He believed that general German enthusiasm for the Holocaust was the result of this hatred.

The Participants

A key question for scholars studying the Holocaust was the role of ideology* in driving mass murder. An innovative approach to this question had been provided by the American historian Christopher Browning. In his 1992 book, *Ordinary Men*, Browning had studied the actions of a German unit named Reserve Police Battalion 101.*

The members of this battalion were mainly middle-aged, working-class Germans, who were either too old for the regular army or who had volunteered for this particular battalion to avoid forced military draft. Browning argued that these ordinary Germans did not carry out the policies of the Holocaust because they felt a particular sense of hatred toward Jews. They did so because of peer pressure. In Browning's words: "Within virtually every social collective, the peer group exerts tremendous pressures on behavior and sets moral norms."[3] Unlike members of the SS* [the elite Nazi paramilitary organization], these men were not trained killers who had been selected especially for their task."

Browning looked at a group of 500 men who were neither hardened Nazi Party members, nor brutalized by war. Nonetheless, when given orders to kill, they murdered 38,000 Jews in the summer of 1942 and sent another 42,500 to the death camps. Browning argued they followed their orders, even if they were sickened by them, out of respect for authority and a desire to fit in with their peers. These psychological motives are not specifically German: they are common to humankind. As a result, Browning insisted that such episodes of horrific violence could happen elsewhere.

The Contemporary Debate

Goldhagen criticized Christopher Browning's argument that ordinary Germans were not personally motivated by anti-Semitism. He believed that anti-Semitic attitudes were pervasive throughout German culture, and that these attitudes dehumanized Jews and made it easy for German soldiers to murder them.

Goldhagen agreed with those who put forward the *Sonderweg* thesis that there was something uniquely toxic about German politics that had led to this generalized national hatred of Jews. He sought to support his case by investigating three particular "institutions" or ideas[4] that were central to the implementation of the Holocaust. These were the police battalions, labor camps, and the death marches* that followed the evacuation of the labor camps in late 1944 and early 1945. In an interview, Goldhagen said he focused on these three elements because "there's been little written about them and because they put to the test my hypothesis and help us understand the motivation of the killers."[5] With his data set identified, Goldhagen then tried to work out the extent to which each institution was influenced by anti-Semitism. This would allow him to "assess [anti-Semitism's] causal efficacy."[6] Given that he was interested in the motivation of ordinary Germans, he deliberately omitted discussion of the extermination camps, which were manned by specially trained and elite Nazi units.

NOTES

1 Zygmunt Bauman, *Modernity and the Holocaust* (Cambridge: Polity, 1989).

2 Daniel Jonah Goldhagen, *Hitler's Willing Executioners: Ordinary Germans and the Holocaust* (New York: Vintage Books, 1997), 49.

3 Christopher Browning, *Ordinary Men: Reserve Police Battalion 101 and the Final Solution in Poland* (New York: HarperCollins, 1992), 3–8.

4 Goldhagen, *Hitler's Willing Executioners*, 467.

5 Daniel Jonah Goldhagen, "How Could They Have Done It?," *Harvard University Gazette*, June 6, 1996.

6 Goldhagen, *Hitler's Willing Executioners*, 467.

MODULE 4
THE AUTHOR'S CONTRIBUTION

KEY POINTS

- Goldhagen claims that German society had produced a virulent form of eliminationist* anti-Semitism.*

- He shifts attention away from elites to reveal the anti-Semitic attitudes of the German masses.

- Goldhagen was original in claiming that popular anti-Semitic attitudes were sufficient to cause the Holocaust,* and in aiming his book at a popular audience.

Author's Aims

When writing *Hitler's Willing Executioners,* Goldhagen had three broad aims. The first was to challenge the American historian Christopher Browning's* "ordinary men" thesis. Browning argued that peer pressure, not ideology, motivated German soldiers to carry out the Holocaust.[1] Browning's conclusion was that anybody, of any nationality, is capable of acting as these men did under circumstances of war. In 1992, Goldhagen reviewed *Ordinary Men* for the American publication *The New Republic.** Strongly rejecting Browning's thesis, he promised to write a book showing that the killing was motivated by an especially vicious and uniquely German form of anti-Semitism.[2]

Goldhagen's second aim was to offer a fundamental reinterpretation of the previous 400 years of German history. This aim is often overlooked in discussions of *Hitler's Willing Executioners.* According to Goldhagen, ever since the sixteenth century the only distinctive feature of German history had been a deeply held and enduring anti-Semitism.[3] He argues that the German monk Martin Luther*—a key figure in the Protestant Reformation,* which created a new branch of

> 66 The conclusion of these chapters is that in Germany during the Nazi period an almost universally held conceptualization of the Jews existed which constituted what can be called an 'eliminationist' ideology, namely the belief that the Jewish influence, by nature destructive, must be eliminated irrevocably from society. 99
>
> Daniel Jonah Goldhagen, *Hitler's Willing Executioners*

Christianity that broke with the Catholic Church—was profoundly anti-Jewish. Luther dominated the Reformation in the German states, and as a result German Protestantism was ingrained with anti-Semitism from the very beginning. Goldhagen then argues that hatred toward Jews* in Germany took on a genocidal form in the nineteenth century. This came about because of the rise of what was known as scientific racism,* which looked to explain differences between humans on the grounds of both biology and ancestry. Scientific racism turned religious prejudice into racial prejudice. Goldhagen wanted to show that anti-Semitism was an essential and long-standing part of German culture and that it had shaped the "eliminationist" way in which German people thought.[4]

Thirdly, Goldhagen aimed to reach and influence a popular audience. He wanted to write a book that would connect with popular debates about how to commemorate the Holocaust in the 1990s.

Approach

The central idea of *Hitler's Willing Executioners* is that ordinary Germans were able to carry out Holocaust policies because of the hatred they felt toward Jews. The Australian historian A. D. Moses* has identified two distinct aspects to Goldhagen's argument: a "minimalist claim" and a "maximalist" one.[5] The minimalist claim simply states that anti-

Semitism was widespread in Nazi* Germany and formed a necessary, if not sufficient, condition for the Holocaust. Moses calls this "reasonable." Goldhagen's maximalist claim argues that Germans felt a unique and genocidal hatred toward Jews,[6] which Moses describes as "extraordinary." According to this claim, the extermination of European Jews was a German national project, so even those who did not directly participate in violence acted as "members of an assenting genocidal community."[7]

Goldhagen was not the first historian to recognize that the Holocaust drew on popular German resentment of Jews. "That the Germans were eager participants: there are any number of books by people who survived which attest to this," wrote the historian Walter Laqueur.*[8] But here Laqueur is addressing the minimalist form of Goldhagen's argument. Goldhagen's maximal claim was not merely that Germans were anti-Semitic: it was that anti-Semitism had been a consistent feature of German culture since the sixteenth century. In addition, the nineteenth-century shift toward a racial (rather than religious) anti-Semitism had resulted in a genocidal form of anti-Jewish feeling.[9] Only in Germany, Goldhagen argues, could the Final Solution* be presented as the fulfillment of a national dream.

Contribution in Context

Goldhagen saw his approach as radically different from that of other historians. In 1988 the Princeton historian Arno J. Mayer* had published a book called *Why Did the Heavens Not Darken?* This argued that the Holocaust had come about because of anti-Communist* feeling in Germany, rather than anti-Semitism. The Jews were believed to be allies of the Communists, who controlled the Soviet Union* and were perceived to be a threat to Germany. Similar arguments had been heard before. In the 1980s German historian Ernst Nolte* had alleged that the Holocaust was a "defensive reaction" to the threat of Communism.[10] In a review of Mayer's book Goldhagen said that references to external societies were an "enormous intellectual error."[11] It was an *internal* hatred that had driven the Holocaust.

Goldhagen also reviewed Christopher Browning's* 1992 book *Ordinary Men*. Highly critical of Browning's conclusions, Goldhagen called his review "The Evil of Banality." In it he challenged Browning's argument that ordinary Germans who carried out the Holocaust were motivated by peer pressure rather than a true hatred of Jews, and that anti-Semitism was largely incidental.[12] Goldhagen wrote *Hitler's Willing Executioners* to demolish Browning's theories and to show that these "ordinary" Germans were gripped by "eliminationist* anti-Semitism." Goldhagen wasn't only interested in debating with scholars, however. He wanted his ideas to reach a wide audience. And while his fellow historians might disagree with him, Goldhagen felt his argument genuinely reflected public opinion.

NOTES

1 Christopher Browning, *Ordinary Men: Reserve Police Battalion 101 and the Final Solution in Poland* (New York: HarperCollins, 1992).

2 Daniel Jonah Goldhagen, "The Evil of Banality," *The New Republic*, July 13 and 20, 1992, 49–52.

3 Daniel Jonah Goldhagen, *Hitler's Willing Executioners: Ordinary Germans and the Holocaust* (New York: Vintage Books, 1997), 53.

4 Goldhagen, *Hitler's Willing Executioners*, 45.

5 A. D. Moses, "Structure and Agency in the Holocaust: Daniel J. Goldhagen and His Critics," *History and Theory* 37, no. 2 (1998): 214.

6 Goldhagen, *Hitler's Willing Executioners*, 49.

7 Goldhagen, *Hitler's Willing Executioners*, 448.

8 Walter Laqueur, quoted in Dinita Smith, "Challenging a View of the Holocaust," *New York Times*, April 1, 1996. Examples of the books Laqueur describes include Holocaust memoirs such as Primo Levi's *If This Is a Man* (1947) and Rudolf Vrba and Alan Bestic's *I Cannot Forgive* (1964).

9 Goldhagen, *Hitler's Willing Executioners*, 65.

10 Ernst Nolte, "Die Vergangenheit, die nicht vergehen will," *Frankfurter Allgemeine Zeitung*, June 6, 1986.

11 Daniel Jonah Goldhagen, "False Witness," *The New Republic*, April 17, 1989, 40.

12 Daniel Jonah Goldhagen, "The Evil of Banality," *The New Republic*, July 13 and 20, 1992, 49–52.

SECTION 2
IDEAS

MODULE 5
MAIN IDEAS

KEY POINTS

- Goldhagen alleges that the German nation welcomed the killing of Jews,* because of their perverse anti-Semitic* ideology.

- Goldhagen believes that a centuries-old form of eliminationist* anti-Semitism existed in German culture.

- The book is written in a highly provocative style. It was produced by a commercial publisher and gained a wide non-specialist readership.

Key Themes

Hitler's Willing Executioners focuses on what motivated the Holocaust* and who or what was responsible for the killing. The book seeks to assess the following:

- The extent to which anti-Semitism was a factor in the Holocaust.
- What form that anti-Semitism took.
- Whether or not that anti-Semitism was unique to Germany.

Daniel Jonah Goldhagen focuses on the people who carried out the Holocaust, the "ordinary" Germans responsible for carrying out mass killings. He believed that nearly all previous scholars of the Holocaust had assumed the German people were either coerced into becoming killers or failed to realize what was happening around them. Goldhagen puts forward the idea that the German people had *chosen* to act. "In contrast to previous scholarship, this book takes the actors' cognition and values seriously and investigates the perpetrators' actions in light of a model of choice."[1]

❝ Whatever the anti-Semitic traditions were in other European countries, it was only in Germany that an openly and rabidly anti-Semitic movement came to power ... that was bent upon turning anti-Semitic fantasy into state organized genocidal slaughter. ❞

Daniel Jonah Goldhagen, *Hitler's Willing Executioners*

Under Nazi* leader Adolf Hitler,* the Germans had committed crimes that ran counter to all norms of civilized behavior. Goldhagen constantly stresses how hard it is for modern readers to enter into the minds of Germans in the 1930s and 1940s. To do so they would need to abandon many of their conventional ideas about human behavior. He argues, "Why not approach Germany as an anthropologist would the world of a people about whom little is known?"[2] Despite the strangeness of the German worldview, it had to be taken and looked at on its own terms if the Holocaust were to be truly understood. Goldhagen's key point is that the crimes of the Holocaust were committed freely, so the German nation as a whole was responsible for the atrocities. "To the very end, the ordinary Germans who perpetrated the Holocaust willfully, faithfully and zealously slaughtered Jews." As an example, Goldhagen highlights the forced death marches,* where many thousands of Jewish prisoners were moved on foot from concentration camps* and prison camps. Many were already horribly weakened by forced labor, but any who could not keep pace were executed. Goldhagen says that the killing of Jews by camp guards and administrators continued on these marches even after the Nazi hierarchy had ordered it to stop.[3]

Exploring the Ideas

The central argument of *Hitler's Willing Executioners: Ordinary Germans and the Holocaust* is that ordinary Germans participated in the

Holocaust because they were motivated by "eliminationist anti-Semitism."[4] Goldhagen argues that this had been the defining feature of the German character since the Protestant Reformation.* At first, the desire had been to make the Jews disappear by converting them to Christianity or by thoroughly assimilating them into German society. In the nineteenth century, however, biological understandings of race began to appear. A number of influential thinkers emerged at this time, arguing that the Jews should be erased from Germany by expulsion, isolation, or, ultimately, extermination. As a result, Goldhagen argues that Hitler's actions reflected the historic wishes of the German people.

Other historians of the Third Reich*—the period of Nazi power in Germany from 1933 to 1945—had alternative explanations for the Holocaust. These included:

- A fear of Communism.* This was advanced by the German historian Ernst Nolte.*
- Increasing radicalization among the Nazi leadership as the war progressed. This argument was associated with functionalist* historians.
- The argument that the killing was predominantly carried out by fanatical Nazi leaders. Many intentionalist* historians had focused on the personal beliefs of Hitler.
- American historian Christopher Browning's* argument that common soldiers were motivated by peer pressure and a fear of disobeying orders.

For Goldhagen, each of these explanations misses a key issue: the fact that Hitler's policies found such wide acclaim and that so many members of the German public went along with them.

To illustrate the link between Nazi policies and ordinary Germans, Goldhagen analyzes three elements: the police battalions— the "agents of genocide*" who carried out countless executions of Jews; the labor camps, in which Jews were enslaved and forced to carry out brutal tasks; and the death marches that took place following the evacuation of the camps.

Goldhagen wanted to find out the extent to which each of these was influenced by anti-Semitism. He relied on the testimony of witnesses and survivors, as well as archival evidence. In each area, Goldhagen claims to have found ample evidence of eliminationist anti-Semitism among German citizens—and claims that this is the dominant cause of the Holocaust: "With regard to the motivational cause of the Holocaust, for the vast majority of perpetrators, a monocausal explanation does suffice."[5]

Language and Expression

The most controversial aspect of *Hitler's Willing Executioners* was Goldhagen's contention that eliminationist anti-Semitism existed, and that it was unique to Germany. This is clearly outlined at the beginning of the book. The rest of the text explores the case studies that, according to Goldhagen, proved his ideas. His conclusion draws on the evidence outlined throughout the book, which he uses to reject prior historical interpretations of the Holocaust and to reassert his own thesis.

Goldhagen presents his ideas in a clear and straightforward manner. Although the book is long and dense, with exhaustive footnotes, *Hitler's Willing Executioners* was written to be accessible to members of the public, as well as to professional historians. It contains a wealth of anecdotal material, and Goldhagen dramatizes the events of the Holocaust in graphic and shocking detail. The book was published by Alfred A. Knopf, a popular rather than academic American publishing company. When it first appeared in 1996, it became an international publishing sensation. Within its first year, it had been translated into 12 languages and had topped best-seller lists around the world, including those of the United States, Britain, and Germany. One important reason for the book's commercial success, especially in America, was what the historian Jane Caplan* has referred to as its "astute prepublication publicity."[6]

NOTES

1   Daniel Jonah Goldhagen, *Hitler's Willing Executioners: Ordinary Germans and the Holocaust* (New York: Vintage Books, 1997), 15.

2   Goldhagen, *Hitler's Willing Executioners*, 28.

3   Goldhagen, *Hitler's Willing Executioners*, 371.

4   Goldhagen, *Hitler's Willing Executioners*, 49.

5   Goldhagen, *Hitler's Willing Executioners*, 416.

6   Jane Caplan, "Reflections on the Reception of Goldhagen in the United States," in *The "Goldhagen Effect": History, Memory, Nazism—Facing the German Past*, ed. Geoff Eley (Ann Arbor: University of Michigan Press, 2000), 154.

MODULE 6
SECONDARY IDEAS

KEY POINTS

- Goldhagen presents German society in the 1930s as being in the grip of a collective delusion, which could not be analyzed through commonsense assumptions.

- He compares his task to that of an anthropologist* and rejects any idea that the Germans were merely indifferent to the fate of the Jews.* In fact, they rejoiced in it.

- Goldhagen also points out the collaboration of the Christian* churches with the Nazis'* anti-Jewish policies.

Other Ideas

Goldhagen's book *Hitler's Willing Executioners* argues for the existence of eliminationist* anti-Semitism* in Germany. In doing this, he makes a bold claim about the root causes of the Holocaust.* Unlike Marxist* historians, who tended to believe that it was social conditions that shaped people's ideas, Goldhagen stresses that it was ideas that shaped the social environment. He insists it was the mental life of the German nation that was decisive in bringing about the Holocaust: the common fears, hopes, and hatreds that underpinned the German national identity. One example of this was the Germans' paranoid belief that all Jews were enemies, which drove the Nazis to embrace total extermination in a "continent-wide project."[1] The idea had no basis in social experience or reality, but it was a fantasy powerful enough to remodel the social order.

Goldhagen claims that previous historians of the Holocaust refused to take these German beliefs seriously "… because the beliefs have seemed to us to be so ridiculous, indeed worthy of the ravings of

❝ Indeed, the corpus of German anti-Semitic literature in the nineteenth and twentieth centuries—with its wild and hallucinatory accounts of the nature of Jews, their virtually limitless power, and their responsibility for nearly every harm that has befallen the world—is so divorced from reality that anyone reading it would be hard pressed to conclude it was anything but the product of the collective scribes of an insane asylum. No aspect of Germany is in greater need of this sort of anthropological reevaluation than is its people's anti-Semitism. ❞

Daniel Jonah Goldhagen, *Hitler's Willing Executioners*

madmen, the truth that they were the common property of the German people has been and will likely continue to be hard to accept by many who are beholden to our common-sense view of the world, or who find the implications of this truth too disquieting."[2]

Goldhagen wants to show that, when it came to Nazi Germany, commonsense ideas did not apply. He emphasizes the Germans' "voluntarism, enthusiasm and cruelty in performing their assigned and self-appointed tasks"[3] and believes that only by paying attention to the *ideas* these people held (what he called the "cognitive explanation") can the Holocaust be fully grasped. These warped beliefs were not just confined to the Nazi Party elites, but were found throughout German society. For Goldhagen, each killer he cites—however extreme their actions or "bizarre" their words—is "representative" or "typical" of a deep German malaise.[4]

Exploring the Ideas

One of Goldhagen's most arresting ideas is his belief in the strangeness of Nazi culture. He insists that German society in the early twentieth century was alien, even exotic. Historians needed to approach their subject with the "critical eye of an anthropologist disembarking on unknown shores, open to meeting a radically different culture."[5] Goldhagen used his own research into the idea of collective psychology to explain the Holocaust. His approach treats the Germans as a single mind or consciousness, ruled by a strange sickness. He cites observers in Warsaw who described the German soldiers as "diseased," "tyrannical," "sadistic"; men and women who were in the grip of "magical thinking."[6] In one telling metaphor, he compares the German obsession with wiping out the Jews to the obsession of Herman Melville's* literary character Captain Ahab, hunting the whale Moby Dick.[7]

Goldhagen argues that this compound of irrational beliefs about the Jews was not created by the Nazis. Hitler exploited hatreds and fears that had been festering for centuries and "allowed" the German people to shake off the last ethical restraints that had held them back: "Germans' beliefs about Jews unleashed indwelling destructive and ferocious passions that are usually tamed and curbed by civilization."[8] Would these feelings have surfaced had Hitler not risen to power in 1933? It's hard to say. But Goldhagen believes that they were commonly shared by German citizens. He says the Germans had actively celebrated the persecution of the Jews. In contrast, the British historian Ian Kershaw* had argued that the Germans were merely indifferent to it. Goldhagen says this was a "virtual psychological impossibility."[9]

Some Germans did speak out against other Nazi policies, like the euthanasia* program that looked to sterilize couples considered "unfit" and to kill people considered to be "defective" in some way. But there was almost no resistance to policies regarding Jews. Goldhagen argues that this was because there were universally negative stereotypes of Jews in German culture. "This is not surprising, for no alternative, institutionally supported public image of the Jews portraying them as human beings was available on which Germans could have drawn."[10]

Overlooked

Goldhagen also emphasizes the compliance of the Christian churches in anti-Jewish violence. As Jews were attacked, the clergy remained largely silent. "The German churches provide a crucial case in the study of the breadth, character and power of modern German eliminationist anti-Semitism, because their leadership and membership could have been expected, for a variety of reasons, to have been among the people in Germany most resistant to it."[11] Christian teaching should have led the churches to show anger against injustice and compassion for the suffering of victims. So the churches' refusal to condemn what was happening emerged from their own moral choice and political beliefs. Both Protestant and Catholic German Christians vilified the Jews in "Nazi-like terms," and the Catholic background of some of the men in Reserve Police Battalion 101* did nothing to hold them back from committing cold-blooded executions.[12] The churches' lack of moral leadership was a clear indicator that "the Nazified conception of Jews and support for the eliminationist project was extremely widespread, a virtual axiom."[13]

The role of the Christian church during the Third Reich* was already a sensitive topic.[14] Goldhagen's critique points out the continuity between religious prejudice against Judaism* (Jews were denounced as the scorners and killers of Christ) and later, biological forms of anti-Semitism (or scientific racism*). Goldhagen associates the Christian faith of the time with anti-Jewish belief, and pushed this claim further in his controversial follow-up book, 2002's *A Moral Reckoning*. Here, he documented the collusion between the church hierarchies and the Third Reich. This generated angry claims that Goldhagen is actually anti-Catholic.[15]

NOTES

1   Daniel Jonah Goldhagen, *Hitler's Willing Executioners: Ordinary Germans and the Holocaust* (New York: Vintage Books, 1997), 414.

2   Goldhagen, *Hitler's Willing Executioners*, 455.

3   Goldhagen, *Hitler's Willing Executioners*, 375.

4   Goldhagen, *Hitler's Willing Executioners*, 4.

5   Goldhagen, *Hitler's Willing Executioners*, 15.

6   Goldhagen, *Hitler's Willing Executioners*, 397, 412.

7   Goldhagen, *Hitler's Willing Executioners*, 398–9.

8   Goldhagen, *Hitler's Willing Executioners*, 397.

9   Goldhagen, *Hitler's Willing Executioners*, 440.

10   Goldhagen, *Hitler's Willing Executioners*, 441.

11   Goldhagen, *Hitler's Willing Executioners*, 438.

12   Goldhagen, *Hitler's Willing Executioners*, 120.

13   Goldhagen, *Hitler's Willing Executioners*, 437–8.

14   Gordon Zahn, *German Catholics and Hitler's Wars: A Study in Social Control* (Indiana: Notre Dame University Press, 1988); Victoria Barnett, *For the Soul of the People: Protestant Protest Against Hitler* (New York: Oxford University Press, 1992).

15   Philip Jenkins, *The New Anti-Catholicism: The Last Acceptable Prejudice* (Oxford: Oxford University Press, 2003), 177–9.

MODULE 7
ACHIEVEMENT

KEY POINTS

- Goldhagen's main argument—that a unique anti-Jewish mindset in Germany caused the Holocaust*—was rejected by most professional historians. But the debate about *why* Goldhagen was wrong was productive.

- Goldhagen's book was a huge publishing success, especially in the newly reunited and democratic Germany.

- Goldhagen's concept of eliminationist* anti-Semitism* is built on dangerous generalizations. It demonizes the German national character.

Assessing the Argument

In his book *Hitler's Willing Executioners,* Daniel Jonah Goldhagen argues that a vicious form of anti-Semitism, unique to Germany, was the motivation for the Holocaust. This anti-Semitism was evident throughout German society, and allowed ordinary men and women to feel happy about killing Jews.* "The inescapable truth is that, regarding Jews, German culture had evolved to the point where an enormous number of ordinary, representative Germans became—and most of the rest of their fellow Germans were fit to be—Hitler's willing executioners."[1]

Goldhagen's ideas reopened the question as to whether anti-Semitism in Germany was a unique phenomenon. It also reopened a debate over the extent to which anti-Semitism motivated the Holocaust. Although the overwhelming majority of historians rejected Goldhagen's conclusions, his work moved the scholarly debate forward. For the previous two or three decades, academics had focused

66 The discourse among scholars, as it has evolved over the centuries, respects certain rules: arguments count, not the people pushing them ... So far, all of the experts in the area of the Holocaust, regardless of their personal background, have been unanimous in severely criticizing Goldhagen's book. That this is the case, fifty years after the fact, and on such a highly emotional and complex subject, is a very hopeful sign. 99

Ruth Bettina Birn, "Historiographical Review: Revising the Holocaust"

on the decision-makers within the Nazi* hierarchy. This meant that the actions of "ordinary" Germans had tended to be overlooked. Goldhagen's book forced scholars to address this.

It also drove academics to think about what kind of arguments and approaches were acceptable within the field of Holocaust studies and the discipline of history more generally. In criticizing Goldhagen's argument, approach, and methodology, a consensus was reached about the process of historical research.

Achievement in Context

Despite widespread scholarly criticism, *Hitler's Willing Executioners* achieved enormous popular success in Europe and America. *Time* magazine* named it one of the two best non-fiction books of 1996, and it was also a finalist for the National Book Critics Circle Award. While it is difficult to generalize about the response in specific nations, the public response seems to have been most favorable in Germany, where the work met with extraordinary media interest. The German weekly *Die Zeit* published a series of reviews by leading historians, followed by a long response to these reviews by Goldhagen himself.[2] Goldhagen also undertook a speaking tour, appearing on German television and in a series of sold-out public debates with prominent German historians. The media frenzy resulted in phenomenal sales: within the first six months of publication, the German translation of *Hitler's Willing Executioners* sold over 160,000 copies.[3]

The book's success in Germany is open to different interpretations. Was the newly reunited nation eager to face up to the burden of past crimes? Or did the book offer modern Germans— whom Goldhagen described as "democrats, committed democrats"—the comfort of thinking their ancestors possessed a mindset that was radically different from their own? Goldhagen presented Germans in the 1930s as having been seized by a collective delirium. Fortunately, he argued, these "absurd beliefs" did not outlive the Nazi regime. Re-education after the war saw the psychotic German hatred of Jews "dissipate."[4] The American political scientist Norman Finkelstein* and the Canadian historian Ruth Bettina Birn* have argued that Goldhagen's thesis, although it was presented as "a searing indictment of Germans, is, in fact, their perfect alibi. After all, who can condemn a 'crazy' people?"[5] Interestingly, the book met with little interest in Israel. There, according to the Israeli historian Shulamit Volkov,* the public reaction was largely indifferent, since it "merely confirms what so many Israelis always 'knew'."[6]

Limitations

Goldhagen emphasizes the unique form that hatred for Jews took in Germany. To do this he uses the evidence of a few case studies to generalize about the mindset of the entire German people. This approach has been hugely controversial. Some historians even accused Goldhagen of anti-German racism.[7] Goldhagen lumps together many different forms of anti-Semitism (religious, racial, exclusionary, eliminationist). He then claims continuity for anti-

Semitism across the centuries, completely overlooking variations in time and place. He argues that eliminationist anti-Semitism had existed since the days of Protestant reformer Martin Luther* and that Hitler had simply harnessed pre-existing hatreds when he came to power in 1933. But if eliminationist anti-Semitism was such a powerful force in German life, why had it not erupted into political life before?

The historian A. D. Moses* has pointed out that *Hitler's Willing Executioners* contributes to another debate: should the Holocaust be interpreted according to a "universalist" or "particularist" narrative? Moses uses the term "universalist" to describe scholars who view the Holocaust in a broad context, and look for links between this and other genocides.* In contrast, particularists understand the Holocaust as a unique and exclusively German and Jewish event. Moses believes that the universalism versus particularism debate is important, but he criticizes Goldhagen for embracing a crude form of particularism.[8]

Subsequent research on the Holocaust has rejected Goldhagen's narrowly German perspective. Scholars have explored anti-Semitism and mass murder in central and Eastern Europe, where the Nazis could count on many ardent collaborators. This research shows that even if eliminationist anti-Semitism existed, it was not restricted to Germany alone. In another move away from a narrowly German perspective, other academics have looked at the connections between colonialism* and the Holocaust. Their argument is that colonialism in Africa and Asia involved wars of conquest, enslavement, and eugenics. The Nazis imported these practices back to Europe, where they sought to create a new land empire on the continent.[9]

NOTES

1   Daniel Jonah Goldhagen, *Hitler's Willing Executioners: Ordinary Germans and the Holocaust* (New York: Vintage Books, 1997), 454.

2   See Bernard Rieger, "'Daniel in the Lion's Den?' The German Debate about Goldhagen's *Hitler's Willing Executioners,*" *History Workshop Journal* 43 (1997): 226–33.

3   John Röhl, "Ordinary Germans as Hitler's Willing Executioners? The Goldhagen Controversy," in *Historical Controversies and Historians*, ed. William Lamont (London: UCL Press, 1998), 16.

4   Goldhagen, *Hitler's Willing Executions*, 593–4.

5   Norman G. Finkelstein and Ruth Bettina Birn, *A Nation on Trial: The Goldhagen Thesis and Historical Truth* (New York: Metropolitan Books, 1998).

6   Shulamit Volkov, quoted in Omer Bartov, "Reception and Perception: Goldhagen's Holocaust and the World," in *The "Goldhagen Effect": History, Memory, Nazism—Facing the German Past*, ed. Geoff Eley (Ann Arbor: University of Michigan Press, 2000), 68.

7   David North, *Anti-Semitism, Fascism and the Holocaust: A Critical Review of Daniel Goldhagen's* Hitler's Willing Executioners (Michigan: Labor Publications, 1996), 5–7.

8   A. D. Moses, "Structure and Agency in the Holocaust: Daniel J. Goldhagen and His Critics," *History and Theory* 37, no. 2 (1998): 194–219.

9   Mark Mazower, *Hitler's Empire: Nazi Rule in Occupied Europe* (London: Penguin, 2008).

MODULE 8
PLACE IN THE AUTHOR'S WORK

KEY POINTS

- Goldhagen is interested in the connection between "eliminationist"* forms of racism and acts of genocide.*

- Goldhagen's later work focused on the Catholic Church and global genocide.

- *Hitler's Willing Executioners* was Goldhagen's breakthrough book, but it was so fiercely attacked by professional historians that it has permanently dented his reputation as a scholar.

Positioning

Daniel Jonah Goldhagen published *Hitler's Willing Executioners* when he was a young scholar, aged 37. It was based on his Harvard doctorate and looked at how and why ordinary people collaborate in genocidal politics. This interest has dominated Goldhagen's scholarly career. His second book, *A Moral Reckoning*, was published in 2002. It discusses the Catholic Church's complicity in the Holocaust*[1] and is thematically and methodologically similar to *Hitler's Willing Executioners*. In *A Moral Reckoning*, Goldhagen argues that the Catholic Church has a long-term history of anti-Semitism.* The failure of the clergy to speak out against Jewish* persecution during the Holocaust contributed to Jewish suffering. These ideas were also expressed in *Hitler's Willing Executioners*.[2]

In 2003, Goldhagen resigned from his professorship at Harvard University to focus on writing. His next book, *Worse Than War: Genocide, Eliminationism, and the Ongoing Assault on Humanity*, was published in 2009. Here, Goldhagen looks at global genocides more

> ❝The Church has a state, vast material holdings, formal diplomacy; it makes treaties of cooperation and has more than one billion adherents. Its doctrine, like the ideology of a state, is political, and it has consequences who are not Catholic. Historically, the Church has been animated by an analogue of aggressive nationalism, preaching exclusivity, a conquering imperialism of the soul, and disdain and hatred of others, particularly Jews. ❞
>
> Daniel Jonah Goldhagen, *A Moral Reckoning: The Role of the Catholic Church in the Holocaust and Its Unfulfilled Duty of Repair*

generally.[3] His focus is on "eliminationism": a deliberate and planned form of genocide based on hatred of a given group.

Goldhagen's latest book, published in 2013, is called *The Devil That Never Dies*.[4] This is about the rise of global anti-Semitism. He has consistently maintained the basic conclusions of *Hitler's Willing Executioners*, extending them to other groups, times, and places.

Integration

The factor that links all Goldhagen's writings is his fascination with the connection between racist hatred and mass murder. He argues against the idea that genocidal violence is the result of short-term triggers or structural factors. Instead, he aims to uncover the deeply held and long-standing beliefs that demonize minorities and provoke fantasies of eliminating them.

Goldhagen believes that eliminationist thinking is not simply a prejudice against a particular ethnic group. He argues that it has a warped moral component, which grows out of Christian beliefs about the existence of evil. In eliminationist thinking, the existence of a hated minority group somehow pollutes the moral order.[5]

Arguing that eliminationism existed in Germany has two strong
political and ethical consequences:

• It implies that the German nation as a whole was collectively
guilty for the Holocaust, because the Holocaust emerged out of a
shared national culture.

• It reveals the continuities between the religiously inspired
persecutions of medieval times and later scientific racism,*
which advanced a similar eliminationist project, even though it
was expressed in different terms. This connection has led
Goldhagen to highlight, repeatedly, what he describes as the
intolerant and destructive behavior of the Christian churches.

In 2009 Goldhagen published his book *Worse Than War*. This
argued that eliminationist thinking could be seen in genocides in
Kenya, Cambodia, and Rwanda.[6] In *Hitler's Willing Executioners*,
Goldhagen had associated eliminationism exclusively with Germans
(as perpetrators) and Jews (as victims). In *Worse Than War* he extends
the idea to any deliberate and planned form of genocide based on
hatred of a given ethnicity, race, or religion. As one reviewer put it,
"*Worse Than War* is, in effect, '*Everyone's Willing Executioners*'."[7]
Broadening the concept of eliminationism has made it more relevant
to scholars in fields like genocide studies, but it also undermines
Goldhagen's claims that there was racism of an exceptional nature in
twentieth-century Germany.

Significance
The phenomenal publishing success of *Hitler's Willing Executioners*
makes it undeniably Goldhagen's most important book. Many senior
historians were dismayed by the work. The German historian
Eberhard Jäckel* dismissed it as "simply a bad book." Another, Hans-
Ulrich Wehler,* said that Goldhagen's views were too sweeping to
be considered scholarly. The American historian István Deák,*

meanwhile, declared in an interview with the *New York Times*, "To say that anti-Semitism is a German speciality is wrong. To say this is somehow a national characteristic is unhistorical."[8]

Yet the book's success meant that scholars were forced to confront its arguments. This led to the so-called "Goldhagen effect": the discussion about the merits and faults of *Hitler's Willing Executioners* produced important insights into the problems of writing about the Holocaust. None of Goldhagen's subsequent work has had anything like the same impact. This is partly because of the near-universal negative response of historians to *Hitler's Willing Executioners*. Goldhagen was attacked for his crude methodology and reductive conclusions—comments that suggested he was not just wrong about the Holocaust, but was also an unsound scholar.

Despite this, the book struck a chord with the general public, partly because it chimed with the "commonsense" view of the Holocaust. The Holocaust survivor and Nobel-Prize Winner Elie Wiesel* said that every German schoolchild should be required to read *Hitler's Willing Executioners*.[9] In an interview about how Germans had received it, Goldhagen said, "As I've gone around the country presenting the book, many survivors have come up to me and said, 'Thank you for writing the book. We've been waiting for 50 years for a book that finally accords with our own experience.'"[10]

Echoing Goldhagen's statement—though from a more critical perspective—the Israeli historian Omer Bartov* declared that Goldhagen was simply "appealing to a public that wants to hear what it already believes."[11] Put simply, the work has been more warmly welcomed by Holocaust survivors than by professional historians. This has put the latter in the difficult position of pointing out that commonsense views, and even individual experience, are not always the most reliable foundation for historical truth.

NOTES

1   Daniel Jonah Goldhagen, *A Moral Reckoning: The Role of the Catholic Church in the Holocaust and Its Unfulfilled Duty of Repair* (New York: Alfred A. Knopf, 2002).

2   Daniel Jonah Goldhagen, *Hitler's Willing Executioners, Ordinary Germans and the Holocaust* (New York: Vintage Books, 1997), 109–10.

3   Daniel Jonah Goldhagen, *Worse Than War: Genocide, Eliminationism, and the Ongoing Assault on Humanity* (New York: Public Affairs, 2009).

4   Daniel Jonah Goldhagen, *The Devil That Never Dies: The Rise and Threat of Global Antisemitism* (London: Little, Brown, 2013).

5   Goldhagen, *Hitler's Willing Executioners*, 38–9.

6   Massacres occurred in Kenya in the 1950s; in Cambodia 1975–9; and in Rwanda in 1994, although there is debate as to whether these mass killings constituted genocide.

7   James Traub, "Patterns of Genocide," *New York Times*, October 15, 2009.

8   Eberhard Jäckel, "Einfach ein schlechtes Buch," *Die Zeit*, May 17, 1996, 39; Hans-Ulrich Wehler, "Wie ein Stachel im Fleisch," *Die Zeit*, May 24, 1996, 40; István Deák, quoted in Dinita Smith, "Challenging a View of the Holocaust," *New York Times*, April 1, 1996.

9   John Röhl, "Ordinary Germans as Hitler's Willing Executioners? The Goldhagen Controversy," in *Historical Controversies and Historians*, ed. William Lamont (London: UCL Press, 1998), 16.

10   Daniel Jonah Goldhagen, "How Could They Have Done It?," *Harvard University Gazette*, June 6, 1996.

11   Omer Bartov, "Ordinary Monsters," *The New Republic*, April 29, 1996, 38.

SECTION 3
IMPACT

MODULE 9
THE FIRST RESPONSES

KEY POINTS

- Goldhagen was criticized for concentrating solely on German anti-Semitism;* for failing to distinguish between the fluctuations in anti-Semitic opinion; for being unoriginal; for producing circular arguments about the causes of anti-Semitic feeling; and for writing sensationalist prose.

- Goldhagen insisted his critics had missed the point and that he had highlighted the role of ideas in causing the Holocaust.*

- The quarrel over *Hitler's Willing Executioners* was embittered by disputes over the Israel–Palestine conflict.*

Criticism

Hitler's Willing Executioners was met with hostility from professional historians. Numerous criticisms were made, the most common being that Goldhagen had grossly oversimplified history. He said there was a single explanation for the Holocaust—widespread anti-Semitism. Historians pointed out that many non-Germans also participated in the Holocaust, including Ukrainians, Lithuanians, Latvians, Poles, French, and Austrians. By focusing exclusively on Germans, Goldhagen was effectively absolving these other nations of any responsibility.[1] They also noted that Goldhagen's argument gave no place to the Germans who had helped Jews* during the Holocaust.[2]

Other scholars criticized Goldhagen's understanding of the role of anti-Semitism in the decades and centuries prior to the Third Reich.* They argued that hatred toward Jews was not the defining feature of German society, as Goldhagen claimed. The history of

66 What is striking among some of those who have criticized my book—against whom so many people in Germany are openly reacting—is that much of what they have written and said has either a tenuous relationship to the book's contents or is patently false. Some of the outright falsehoods include: that little is new in the book; that it puts forward a monocausal and deterministic explanation of the Holocaust, holding it to have been the inevitable outcome of German history; that its argument is ahistorical; and that it makes an 'essentialist,' 'racist' or ethnic argument about Germans. None of these is true.**99**

Daniel Jonah Goldhagen, "Motives, Causes and Alibis"

anti-Semitism in countries like France, Russia, and Austria was arguably much worse than in Germany. According to the Israeli historian Yehuda Bauer,* "There simply was no general murderous, racist, antisemitic norm in Germany in the nineteenth century ... To speak of an eliminationist norm is wrong. Goldhagen's thesis does not work."[3] The British historian Geoff Eley* echoed this point, arguing that Goldhagen's "argument failed to explain why so little legislative discrimination, let alone physical violence, occurred against Jews in Germany before 1914."[4]

Hitler's Willing Executioners was also attacked for lacking originality. Critics like the American political scientist Norman Finkelstein* said that most of its arguments were already known to historians.[5] Historians had already demonstrated that ordinary men and women participated in the killings, that most were not members of the Nazi* Party, and that many had some knowledge of the Final Solution.*[6] The German historian Hans Mommsen,* summarizing these criticisms, declared that the book "falls behind the current state of research, rests on insufficient foundations, and provides no new insights."[7] In a different vein, the German sociologist Y. Michal Bodemann* claimed that Goldhagen's graphic descriptions of violence constituted a "voyeurist narration." He dismissed *Hitler's Willing Executioners* as a "pornography of horror."[8]

Responses

Goldhagen vehemently rejected the negative scholarly response to *Hitler's Willing Executioners*. In numerous publications, both academic and popular, he argued that his views had been misrepresented and, at times, even misquoted. In the afterword to the first paperback edition of *Hitler's Willing Executioners*, he argued that his critics "were not discussing the book's findings, arguments, and conclusions, but rather were raising a series of false issues."[9] He said he felt vindicated that "Most seem now to agree that anti-Semitism was a necessary cause of the Holocaust."[10]

The most heated exchanges were with long-term critics. The Canadian historian Ruth Bettina Birn* reviewed *Hitler's Willing Executioners* and pointed out its many factual errors. In a 47-page response, Goldhagen accused her of "wholesale invention."[11] Following that, Birn and the American political scientist Norman Finkelstein* published *A Nation on Trial: The Goldhagen Thesis and Historical Truth*, which accused Goldhagen of anti-German racism.[12] This confrontation became particularly polemical because Goldhagen accused Finkelstein of being a supporter of the militant Palestinian group Hamas.* As a result, the debate over the Holocaust became entangled with the Israeli–Palestinian conflict. Goldhagen's claims for the unviable situation of Jews in central Europe was interpreted by Finkelstein as an implicit justification for Zionism,* the ideology that defends the project of Jewish resettlement in the ancestral lands of the Old Testament.* In turn, Goldhagen was quick to accuse some of his critics of being motivated by an aggressive anti-Israel agenda.[13]

Conflict and Consensus

The critical dialogue that followed the publication of *Hitler's Willing Executioners* did not persuade either side to make significant changes to their original positions. Goldhagen made no revisions to his central thesis, and the two books he has published since *Hitler's Willing Executioners* built on aspects of his earlier work. He continues to claim that his chief target in the book was the American historian Christopher Browning's* depiction of the "ordinary men" who carried out the Holocaust. Goldhagen insists that "the unreal images of them as isolated, frightened, thoughtless beings performing their tasks reluctantly are erroneous."[14]

Browning, in response, declared that *Hitler's Willing Executioners* oversimplified the Holocaust. In doing so it pandered to a public that said, "We don't want complex answers, we just want an answer. We want to understand the Holocaust as we did fifty years ago— German culture is evil, it created evil people, who committed evil deeds."[15] Browning's point is that historical scholarship has moved on, and that Goldhagen's ideas reflect outmoded ways of understanding both the Holocaust and German history more generally. Indeed, Goldhagen's argument seems to provide an updated version of the old *Sonderweg** ("special path") thesis that circulated immediately after the World War II,* which had suggested that Germany had to be looked at as a case apart.

NOTES

1   David Schoenbaum, "Ordinary People?," *National Review* 48, July 1, 1996.

2   Steve Aschheim, "Archetypes and the German Jewish Dialogue: Reflections Occasioned by the Goldhagen Affair," *German History* 15, no. 2 (1997): 240–50.

3   Yehuda Bauer, *Rethinking the Holocaust* (New Haven, CT: Yale University Press, 2000), 100.

4 Geoff Eley, "Ordinary Germans, Nazis, and Judeocide," in *The "Goldhagen Effect": History, Memory, Nazism—Facing the German Past*, ed. Geoff Eley (Ann Arbor: University of Michigan Press, 2000), 5–6.

5 Norman Finkelstein, "Daniel Jonah Goldhagen's Crazy Thesis: A Critique of *Hitler's Willing Executioners*," in *New Left Review* 1, no. 224, July–August 1997.

6 For instance, Lucy Davidowicz, *War Against the Jews* (New York: Holt, Rinehart and Winston, 1975).

7 Hans Mommsen, "Die dünne Patina der Zivilisation," *Die Zeit*, August 30, 1996, 14.

8 Y. Michal Bodemann, "Die Bösen und die ganz normalen Guten," *Die Tageszeitung*, August 7, 1996.

9 Daniel Jonah Goldhagen, *Hitler's Willing Executioners: Ordinary Germans and the Holocaust* (New York: Vintage Books, 1997), 463.

10 Daniel Jonah Goldhagen, "A Reply to My Critics," *The New Republic*, December 23, 1996.

11 Daniel Jonah Goldhagen, "The Fictions of Ruth Bettina Birn," *German Politics and Society* 15 (1997): 119–65.

12 Norman G. Finkelstein and Ruth Bettina Birn, *A Nation on Trial: The Goldhagen Thesis and Historical Truth* (New York: Metropolitan Books, 1998).

13 Dominique Vidal, "From *Mein Kampf* to Auschwitz," *Le Monde Diplomatique*, October 1998; Finkelstein, "Daniel Jonah Goldhagen's Crazy Thesis," 39–87.

14 Goldhagen, *Hitler's Willing Executioners*, 406.

15 Christopher Browning, quoted in A. D. Moses, "Structure and Agency in the Holocaust: Daniel J. Goldhagen and His Critics," *History and Theory* 37, no. 2 (1998): 196.

THE EVOLVING DEBATE

KEY POINTS

- Historians are now looking at how the Holocaust* emerged in Europe as a whole.

- The major impact of *Hitler's Willing Executioners* was to launch a useful debate about historical methods and to foster democratic attitudes in modern Germany.

- The work of the Israeli historian Alon Confino* shows some continuity with Goldhagen. Like Goldhagen, Confino wants to understand the anti-Semitic* mentality of the Nazis.*

Uses and Problems

The academic attitude toward *Hitler's Willing Executioners* has remained consistently critical. Contemporary debate about the Holocaust has moved on from the psychological questions of motivation and intentionality raised by the work. It now focuses on larger issues, such as how the mass murder of the Jews* might fit into broader instances of genocide.*[1] This approach directly rejects Goldhagen's primary thesis—that the Holocaust was an exclusively German phenomenon, resulting from a unique form of anti-Semitism.[2]

One particularly fruitful line of research has highlighted links between genocide and imperialism.* In the late nineteenth century, European nations justified their takeover of foreign territories— sometimes leading to the extinction of native peoples—through appeals to what they claimed was a historical and racial destiny. The British academic Mark Mazower* is among several leading historians who have pointed out that the Nazis were trying to carve out an empire of their own in Eastern Europe.[3] This project took its ideas

66 To be sure, had the Germans not found European
(especially Eastern European) helpers, then the
Holocaust would have unfolded somewhat differently,
and the Germans would likely not have succeeded in
killing as many Jews. Still, this was above all a German
enterprise: the decisions, plans, organizational resources
and majority of its executors were German. 99

Daniel Jonah Goldhagen, *Hitler's Willing Executioners*

from earlier European incursions into Africa, which had seen forced
resettlement, racial hierarchies and special forms of detention,
including concentration camps.* In relating imperialism to the
Holocaust, historians have become particularly interested in German
South-West Africa (today's Namibia). In 1909 a rebellion by the
indigenous Herero and Namaqua peoples led the German
authorities there to use extremely brutal methods of punishment.
Some scholars have seen this as anticipating the genocidal policies
against the Jews.[4] The Nazis used the logic of imperialism in Europe
itself. They colonized Eastern Europe in precisely the same manner
that Europeans had previously colonized most of the world.[5]

Schools of Thought

There are no contemporary disciples of *Hitler's Willing Executioners*.
Few, if any, current historians would identify themselves with the
work. The scholarly response dismissed Goldhagen's central theses so
comprehensively that his ideas have faded from contemporary
relevance. Those who defend the book do so largely on the basis of
its provocative power to raise questions, rather than its ability to
provide satisfactory answers. As the Canadian academic Robert
Gellately* has suggested, "Goldhagen had forcefully presented some
challenging insights, offered new and important evidence, and

certainly given us good reason to revise some of our perceptions and understandings."[6]

If Goldhagen's term "eliminationist* anti-Semitism" is helpful at all, it is in relation to the outlook of the Nazi leaders, many of whom expressed no remorse when they were put on trial and confronted with their crimes.[7] Applying the term to the German nation as a whole throws up much more uncertainty. It led Goldhagen into generalizations that were difficult to support. He argued that the German people supported the Nazi regime because they sympathized with its policies. One example of recent scholarship that rejects this is research on the Nazi police and their use of terror. This has shown that many ordinary Germans were coerced into supporting the regime simply out of fear.[8]

In Germany, Goldhagen's work has been seen as an important tool for introducing the next generation to the terrible lessons of the past. When Goldhagen was awarded the Democracy Prize in 1997, the *Journal for German and International Politics* praised him for reminding Germans that they must not abandon the "founding principles of the Federal Republic of Germany." These founding principles sought to ensure that human rights and dignity would always be central to the republic, and that a dictator could never again rise to power in Germany. The *Journal*'s editorial board also referred to the culture of silence about the Holocaust that had predominated in postwar Germany. They paid tribute to Goldhagen for helping young Germans understand the events of the Final Solution,* noting that "as a rule, parents and grandparents had denied them" any answers on the subject.[9]

In Current Scholarship

Goldhagen emphasizes how ideas can lead to mass killing. This line of inquiry has been taken up again recently in the work of the Israeli historian Alon Confino. Like Goldhagen, Confino is interested in the power of ideology and mindsets. He is particularly interested in the fantasy of a "world without Jews." He argues that certain symbolic attacks on German Jews during the early years of the Third Reich* demonstrated a desire to erase Jewish presence from German culture. Most important here was the organized burning of the Jewish scripture, the Torah, in 1938. Through destroying this holy text— what Confino calls "bibliocide"— ordinary Germans believed that they could wipe out Jews from German history.[10]

There are many subtle connections between Goldhagen and Confino. Both are interested in the religious origins of anti-Semitism and how this religious prejudice fed into later, irrational beliefs about the Jews. Both argue that the desire to get rid of the Jews was evident before World War II* and that it was linked to a desire to somehow redeem German history. Both wanted to show that popular ideas were crucial in bringing about the Holocaust. For Confino, scholars "cannot understand why the Nazis persecuted and exterminated the Jews unless we are ready to explore Nazi fantasies, hallucinations and imagination."[11] This emphasis on mentality has once again been controversial. The British historian Richard Evans* has accused Confino of lacking empirical proof for his theses and of overstating the role of religion in formulating prejudice. Evans also criticizes Confino for treating the Germans as a block, "as if all Germans were Nazis and anti-Semites … time and again an argument about 'some Germans' expands within a few pages to become simply 'Germans.'"[12]

NOTES

1   Manus Midlarsky, *The Killing Trap: Genocide in the Twentieth Century* (Cambridge: Cambridge University Press, 2005).

2   Inga Clendinnean, "The Men in the Green Tunics," in *Reading the Holocaust* (Cambridge: Cambridge University Press, 1998): 133–55.

3   Mark Mazower, *Hitler's Empire: Nazi Rule in Occupied Europe* (London: Penguin, 2008).

4   Isabel Hull, *Absolute Destruction: Military Culture and the Practices of War in Imperial Germany* (Ithaca: Cornell University Press, 2006); David Olusoga and Casper Erichsen, *The Kaiser's Holocaust: Germany's Forgotten Genocide and the Colonial Roots of Nazism* (London: Faber and Faber, 2011).

5   Volker Langbehn, Mohammad Salama, eds., *German Colonialism: Race, the Holocaust and Postwar Germany* (New York: Columbia University Press, 2013).

6   Robert Gellateley, "Review: *Hitler's Willing Executioners: Ordinary Germans and the Holocaust*," in *Journal of Modern History* 69, no.1 (1997): 191.

7   Nick Zangwill, "Perpetrator Motivation: Some Reflections on the Goldhagen/ Browning Debate," in *Moral Philosophy and the Holocaust,* ed. Eve Garrard and Geoffrey Scarre (Basingstoke: Ashgate, 2003), 92.

8   Erik Johnson, *Nazi Terror: The Gestapo, Jews and Ordinary Germans* (New York: Basic Books, 2000).

9   Quoted in Debra Bradley Ruder, "Goldhagen Wins German Prize for Holocaust Book," *Harvard University Gazette*, January 9, 1997.

10 Alon Confino, *A World Without Jews: The Nazi Imagination from Persecution to Genocide* (New Haven, London: Yale University Press, 2014).

11 Alon Confino, "Fantasies about the Jews: Cultural Reflections on the Holocaust," *History & Memory* 17 (2005): 297.

12 Richard Evans, "Written into History," *London Review of Books* 37, no. 2 (January 22, 2015): 19.

MODULE 11
IMPACT AND INFLUENCE TODAY

KEY POINTS

- Goldhagen's book has been largely discredited. His focus on ideas has been superseded by interest in the administrative challenge of governing the Nazi* empire.

- The Israeli historian Alon Confino* and the British historian Dan Stone* have adapted some of Goldhagen's arguments.

- Scholars like the American historian Timothy Snyder* and the Polish-American historian Jan Gross* have studied the Holocaust* in the wider context of mass killing in Eastern Europe at the time.

Position

Hitler's Willing Executioners was one of the most talked-about, even infamous, history books of the 1990s. Daniel Jonah Goldhagen's powerful, simple narrative connected with a wide public. The hostility that historians felt toward its arguments forced many of them to publish reviews and articles rejecting Goldhagen's conclusions. Yet many historians feel that this debate was beneficial, because it prompted broad reflection on legitimate ways of writing about the Holocaust.[1]

Goldhagen insisted that collective prejudice played a role in the Holocaust. This has been largely accepted: most historians today would say that these collective passions were a necessary cause of the Holocaust, although they were not the only one. The most sophisticated recent account of the Holocaust, written by the German historian Peter Longerich,* claims that the killing was the result of the

> **❝** Heirs to this tradition, the Nazis shared that imperial desire but did something with it that was shocking to the European mind of the early twentieth century: they tried to build their empire in Europe itself and, what is more, to do it at breakneck speed in only a few years. **❞**

Mark Mazower, *Hitler's Empire: Nazi Rule in Occupied Europe*

interplay between many different causes.[2] He splits Nazi racial policy into two strands: positive and negative. Positive policy sought to exalt the German people and allow them to demonstrate their racial superiority through culture and war. Negative policy aimed to eliminate anything that blocked this vision. Longerich emphasizes that policies against Jews* were issued, at first, as broad principles. This allowed for a large element of creative enforcement by bureaucrats and local officials. He references *Kristallnacht,** "The Night of Broken Glass" in November 1938, in which Jewish people and properties were attacked. While a few thousand Germans passionately participated in these attacks, most stayed passive and silent. Longerich argues that the outbreak of war accelerated the Nazis' pursuit of both positive and negative racial policies. There was no single turning point at which the idea of exterminating the Jews was proclaimed. Rather, systematic killing emerged out of a host of disparate local efforts to solve what the Nazis saw as the Jewish problem. Longerich's analysis is a far more complex and subtle account than Goldhagen's—even if, unlike Goldhagen, he does not deal with the perspective of the actual perpetrators.[3]

Interaction

Goldhagen focused on anti-Semitism* as an aspect of German culture. Other historians have also explored how prevailing cultural beliefs played a role in the Holocaust. The Israeli historian Alon Confino has tried to reconstruct the moment when the Holocaust became "thinkable."[4] The British historian Dan Stone, meanwhile, argued that the Nazis tried to somehow change reality so that it would fit with their beliefs: he believes that the Holocaust can be grasped "as the outcome of a German narrative through which the perpetrators made sense of the world."[5] These scholars want to understand German mental attitudes, but they also insist that the Holocaust should be viewed in a wider European or even a global perspective. This has been implicitly recognized by Goldhagen; in his 2009 book *Worse Than War* he explores genocides* elsewhere in the world.[6]

Today's leading scholarship underlines the decisive role of Germany's allies in the Holocaust. When Hungary annexed parts of Czechoslovakia, the Jews living there were expelled. This created a refugee problem for the Germans, which they solved by mass murder.[7] In his book *Neighbours*, the Polish-American historian Jan Gross* reconstructed the murder of Jews in a Polish town called Jedwabne. They were killed by the Polish men and women they had lived alongside for generations. Gross reveals how the impact of invasion and occupation allowed a host of bitter grievances to flare up. Eliminationist* anti-Semitism was not a coherent ideology in these circumstances, but rather was mixed with jealousy, greed, opportunism, and fear.[8] Goldhagen had presented the Holocaust as being driven by German thinking. Most scholars today recognize it as a more diffuse process, with many local variants and many non-German collaborators.

The Continuing Debate

Recent works on the Nazi Empire have not simply focused on the Holocaust as a horrific event. For example, there has been investigation into the callous brutality of the 1941 *Generalplan Ost** ("general plan for the east"). Thirty million people would simply be starved to death as food was transferred from Eastern Europe back to the German heartlands. Then the remaining populations would be enslaved, deported, or murdered.[9] The plan was not fully executed, but it demonstrates how far genocide had become a central pillar of Nazi policy in the east. It was not simply aimed at Jews. Slavs, gypsies, ethnic Germans, and millions of Soviet prisoners of war perished in this mass bloodletting.[10]

The American historian Timothy Snyder* has looked at the links between geography and genocide. In his prize-winning book of 2010, *Bloodlands*, Snyder demonstrated that the vast majority of the killing in early twentieth-century Europe was located at the troubled eastern boundaries of the continent.[11] Countries like Poland, the Baltic States, Belarus, and the Ukraine were territories that had previously belonged to the Hapsburg,* Ottoman,* or Russian Empires. These empires had disintegrated during World War I,* leading to political instability, ethnic tension, and vulnerable minority groups. In contrast to Goldhagen, Snyder downplays the importance of ideology. Killing occurred in these areas under various political regimes. What unleashed it was the fragile sense of place. Snyder estimates that 14 million non-combatants were killed between 1933 and 1945 as a result of the reshaping of borders in Eastern Europe. The vast majority of these people did not die in labor or concentration camps.* Snyder is not directly contradicting Goldhagen, but his work shows the benefits of adopting a wider perspective, rather than focusing simply on the clash between Germans and Jews.

NOTES

1   Robert Gellateley, "Review: *Hitler's Willing Executioners: Ordinary Germans and the Holocaust*," *Journal of Modern History* 69, no.1 (1997): 191.

2   Peter Longerich, *Holocaust: The Nazi Persecution and Murder of the Jews* (Oxford: Oxford University Press, 2010).

3   Timothy Snyder, "A New Approach to the Holocaust," *New York Review of Books*, June 23, 2011.

4   Alon Confino, *Foundational Pasts: The Holocaust as Historical Understanding* (Cambridge: Cambridge University Press, 2013), 124.

5   Dan Stone, "Holocaust Historiography and Cultural History," in *The Holocaust and Historical Methodology* (New York: Bergahan, 2012), 56.

6   Daniel Jonah Goldhagen, *Worse than War: Genocide, Eliminationism and the Ongoing Assault on Humanity* (New York: Public Affairs, 2009).

7   Holly Case, *Between States: The Transylvanian Question and the European Idea during World War II* (Stanford: Stanford University Press, 2008).

8   Jan Gross, *Neighbours: The Destruction of the Jewish Community in Jedwabne, Poland* (Princeton: Princeton University Press, 2001).

9   Stephen Fritz, *Ostkrieg: Hitler's War of Extermination in the East* (Kentucky: University of Kentucky Press, 2011).

10 Mark Mazower, *Hitler's Empire: Nazi Rule in Occupied Europe* (London, New York: Penguin, 2008).

11 Timothy Snyder, *Bloodlands: Europe Between Hitler and Stalin* (New York: Basic Books, 2010).

MODULE 12
WHERE NEXT?

KEY POINTS

- The academic impact of *Hitler's Willing Executioners* will probably continue to dwindle and be replaced by more transnational perspectives.

- The importance of *Hitler's Willing Executioners* is partly due to its success in Germany, where it played a role in modern Germany's process of coming to terms with its Nazi* past.

- The text is seminal because of the public controversy it generated among historians and its appeal to the general public.

Potential

In all likelihood, the empirical* conclusions of *Hitler's Willing Executioners* will fade from prominence. The book was published less than 20 years ago, but its influence and relevance have already begun to wane. There are two main reasons for this. The first is that the scholarly reception of the book was resoundingly negative. Almost all of Goldhagen's primary claims were rejected as either incorrect or lacking in originality.[1]

The second reason is that approaches to the Holocaust* and to genocide* studies have moved on since Goldhagen's book was published. Rather than focusing on specific nations and peoples, recent scholarship has emphasized the transnational status of violence in Eastern Europe and the colonial* context of that violence. According to historians like British academic Mark Mazower* and Italian academic Enzo Traverso,* the massacres in Eastern Europe are best understood as the logic of imperialism* turned against Europe itself.[2]

❝ The study of the Holocaust's perpetrators thus provides a window through which German society can be viewed and examined in a new light. It demands that important features of the society be conceived anew. It suggests further that the Nazis were the most profound revolutionaries of modern times and that the revolution that they wrought during their but brief suzerainty [overlordship] in Germany was the most extreme and thoroughgoing in the history of western civilization. It was, above all, a cognitive-moral revolution which reversed processes that had been shaping Europe for centuries. **❞**

Daniel Jonah Goldhagen, *Hitler's Willing Executioners*

But it is unlikely that *Hitler's Willing Executioners* will be entirely forgotten. The book's commercial success revealed the potential of history to inspire the popular imagination, and in fact there has already been a shift away from looking at Goldhagen's ideas to exploring his work as an object of controversy. An edited collection of essays, *The "Goldhagen Effect,"* was published in 2000. This assessed the debate surrounding *Hitler's Willing Executioners*. The respected British historian Geoff Eley* wrote the introductory essay; after subjecting Goldhagen's ideas to intense criticism, he noted that the status of *Hitler's Willing Executioners* as a "public event" is where "its lasting positive value may be found."[3]

Future Directions

The general argument of *Hitler's Willing Executioners* has been largely dismantled. However, some of the themes that Goldhagen highlighted have been explored in subsequent scholarship in a more subtle manner. Goldhagen rejected the notion of Nazi killing as impersonal or mechanistic. He wanted to investigate the *choices* made by the killers: their desire to obey orders and the cruelty they inflicted on their Jewish* victims.[4] This insight has been followed up in the work of the American historian Timothy Snyder.* Snyder has highlighted the crude brutality of the violence against the Jews. In contrast to the "assembly-line killing" of the gas chambers, much of the violence was visceral and intimate—it was inflicted by close-range shooting or physical beatings and torture.[5] While historians need to think hard about the ideas and feelings that could motivate such savage actions, atrocities elsewhere in the world make it impossible to suggest that the violence was due to a uniquely German mentality.

Goldhagen argues that German anti-Semitism—which he characterized as centuries old—suddenly evaporated with the fall of Nazi leader Adolf Hitler.* He struggled to explain this argument convincingly: the transition seemed too sharp to be credible. Subsequent historical research has emphasized how violence persisted after 1945. Europe remained a "savage continent" for several years after the fall of the Third Reich.* Jews who returned home from the camps became victims of theft, beatings, and murder.[6]

Yet another of Goldhagen's allegations might have been correct. Knowledge of the Holocaust was probably more widespread among ordinary Germans than is commonly assumed. This gives added significance to the question of silence on the Holocaust within Germany during the middle decades of the twentieth century. Was it denied? Repressed? Even hidden? Understanding how the perpetrators of the Holocaust were able to adjust to postwar society is a key issue for contemporary research into historical memory.[7] The popular reception of Goldhagen's book in Germany is one chapter in that unfolding story.[8]

Summary

Hitler's Willing Executioners is a peculiar candidate for consideration as a seminal text in modern history. Few works have been greeted with such uniform hostility by scholars within the field. Goldhagen's central ideas and methodological approach have been comprehensively dismissed by historians. The book inspires no school of thought and has had no significant impact on other academic disciplines. Few, if any, current historians would identify themselves with the work. In all likelihood, the ideas contained within it will continue to fall from prominence among academic historians.

But the book was an incredible commercial and popular success. It rose to the top of best-seller lists around the world, turned Goldhagen into a global celebrity, and provoked a furious scholarly debate. Numerous essays have been published exploring the "Goldhagen Controversy."[9] It is because of this, rather than the validity or otherwise of Goldhagen's sources or findings, that the text deserves special attention. Nearly 20 years after its publication, it remains an enlightening case in the history of academic controversies. The ideas of *Hitler's Willing Executioners* are unlikely to influence future historical research. But the book's status as a "public event" means it is likely to be remembered as important for many years to come.[10]

NOTES

1   Hans-Ulrich Wehler, "The Goldhagen Controversy: Agonizing Problems, Scholarly Failure and the Political Dimension," in *German History* 15, no.1 (1997): 80–91.

2   Mark Mazower, *Hitler's Empire: Nazi Rule in Occupied Europe* (London: Penguin, 2008); Enzo Traverso, *The Origins of Nazi Violence*, trans. Janet Lloyd (New York: New Press, 2003).

3   Geoff Eley, "Ordinary Germans, Nazis, and Judeocide," in *The "Goldhagen Effect": History, Memory, Nazism—Facing the German Past*, ed. Geoff Eley (Ann Arbor: University of Michigan Press, 2000), 21.

4   Daniel Jonah Goldhagen, *Hitler's Willing Executioners*: *Ordinary Germans and the Holocaust* (New York: Vintage Books, 1997), 10, 15, 17.

5   Timothy Snyder, "Holocaust: The Ignored Reality," *New York Review of Books*, July 16, 2009.

6 Keith Lowe, *Savage Continent: Europe in the Aftermath of World War II*
   (London, New York: Viking, 2012); Jan Gross, *Fear: Anti-Semitism in Poland
   after Auschwitz: An Essay in Historical Interpretation* (Princeton: Princeton
   University Press, 2006).

7 Jeffrey Herf, *Divided Memory: Nazi Past in the Two Germanys* (Cambridge,
   MA: Harvard University Press, 1997).

8 Klaus Neumann, *Shifting Memories: The Nazi Past in the New Germany*
   (Michigan: University of Michigan Press, 2000).

9 A number of these essays were collected in two important volumes:
   *The "Goldhagen Effect": History, Memory, Nazism—Facing the German
   Past*, ed. Geoff Eley (Ann Arbor: University of Michigan Press, 2000);
   and *Unwilling Germans? The Goldhagen Debate*, ed. Robert R. Shandley
   (Minneapolis: University of Minnesota Press, 1998).

10 Eley, "Ordinary Germans, Nazis, and Judeocide," 21.

GLOSSARY

GLOSSARY OF TERMS

Anthropologist: a person who engages in the scientific study of human beings and culture.

Anti-Semitism: a prejudice against Jews as a people. Anti-Semitism is often distinguished from anti-Judaism, which discriminates against Jews on the basis of their religious beliefs.

Auschwitz: a network of concentration camps and extermination camps built by Nazi Germany in occupied Poland during World War II. It is estimated that 1.1 million Jews were murdered there between 1942 and 1945.

Christian: a follower of Christianity, a major religion based on the life and teachings of Jesus Christ in the first century C.E.

Colonialism: control by one country over another, generally for the purpose of economic exploitation.

Communism: an ideology that aims to abolish private property, put an end to capitalism, and create an egalitarian society. Communism was the official system of the Soviet Union.

Concentration camp: a camp where non-military, perceived enemies of the state are detained in poor conditions and often without trial. Generally associated with the Nazi regime in World War II, where camps held Jews and other persecuted minorities such as homosexuals, gypsies and communists, using them to provide forced labor. Detainees were later executed in large numbers.

Death marches: marches that took place to evacuate Nazi labor and extermination camps. Most of these camps were located in Eastern Europe, particularly Poland. When the Soviet Red Army began to turn the tide of World War II and advance toward Germany through the east, the Nazis evacuated the camps. Camp inmates, already severely weakened and ill after their experiences there, were forced to march for days at a time through freezing terrain. Those who could not keep up were shot and left by the road.

Eastern Front: refers to German campaigns to the east during World War II—first the invasion of Poland in 1939, then the invasion of the Soviet Union under Operation Barbarossa in the summer of 1941. The drive east saw not only huge military losses on the battlefield, but also the systematic murder of civilians.

Eliminationist anti-Semitism: coined by Goldhagen himself, this term describes the goal of removing Jews from society. This can be achieved by a variety of means (conversion, assimilation, expulsion, extermination), but the unifying idea is to ensure that Jews disappear.

Empiricism/Empirical approach: the idea that all knowledge should be gained by experience, by using experiments and observation to gather facts.

Euthanasia: a Nazi program that was a key part of their eugenics agenda, which sought to sterilize unfit couples and murder citizens deemed to be biologically defective, mentally ill, or disabled. Interrupted by criticism from the Catholic Church many of the doctors involved later assisted in advising on the murder of Jews.

Final Solution: a synonym for the Holocaust. The Nazi Party's elite saw the Holocaust as the "final solution to the Jewish problem."

Functionalism: a term used to describe a viewpoint held by some historians during the 1970s and 1980s in the debate over the origins of the Holocaust. Functionalist historians like Hans Mommsen tended to emphasize that there was nothing inevitable about the genocide. Rather, it happened in response to specific structural problems in the Nazi regime—whether that was managing the annexed new territory during the war, or radicalization caused by competing government departments.

Generalplan Ost: means "general plan for the east." This was a secret Nazi plan developed from 1939 to 1942, outlining the future of Eastern Europe after its conquest. It involved the forced starvation, deportation, and ultimately extermination of millions of Slavs, Poles, Jews, and Soviet prisoners.

Genocide: the systematic and willful destruction of a racial, religious, or ethnic group.

Hamas: a militant Palestinian organization, whose military wing has spearheaded the armed resistance to the Israeli occupation of Palestine.

Hapsburg Empire: the territories ruled over by the Hapsburg dynasty, which controlled large parts of central Europe for centuries. With its capital in Vienna, the Empire grew to include Hungary, Bohemia, Slovakia, Slovenia, and Croatia. The Empire collapsed following military defeat in 1918.

Historikerstreit: literally translated as "historians' quarrel," this refers to a fierce controversy in German scholarship in the 1980s. It was triggered by the work of Ernst Nolte, who claimed that the Holocaust needed to be seen as a defensive move against feared killings by the Soviet Union—Germany argued that the Jews were Soviet allies.

Nolte also urged historians to try to feel empathy for the German soldiers fighting on the Eastern Front and to try to see the war through their eyes.

Historiography: the study of how a historical debate evolves over time.

The Holocaust: refers to the systematic murder of roughly six million Jews along with non-Jewish persecuted minorities in Europe by Nazi Germany and her allies. When exactly the Holocaust began remains a subject of great controversy, but most historians agree that the majority of the killing occurred in the years 1941–5.

Holocaust denial: the view of those who claim that either the Holocaust did not happen, or that it happened on a much smaller scale than is typically discussed in the historiography. It is a view linked to many Nazi sympathizers, and tends to lead to conspiracy theories as to how lies about the Holocaust have been manufactured and subsequently accepted. Holocaust denial is a crime in several European states.

Ideology: the cluster of beliefs, values, and goals that underpin social and political movements. Ideology often works at the level of unconscious assumptions, rather than explicit propositions. Racial ideology was at the heart of Nazism in Germany.

Imperialism: refers to the ideology and practice of conquering and ruling over foreign states. Imperialism is the policy that endorses and encourages the creation of empires.

Intentionalism: a term that describes a viewpoint held by certain historians during the 1970s and 1980s in the debate over the origins of the Holocaust. Intentionalist historians tended to stress that the destruction of the Jews was a key part of the Nazi leadership's plan from the beginning. So the Holocaust developed out of the ideology of Hitler and his unwavering objective to solve what was termed the "Jewish question."

Israel–Palestine conflict: the ongoing struggle and wide-ranging conflict between Israelis and Palestinians that began in the mid-twentieth century with the creation of the state of Israel. It is based mainly on conflicting issues of nationalism and territory.

Jews: a follower of the religion of Judaism and member of the Semitic community descended from the ancient Hebrew people of Israel.

Judaism: monotheistic religion founded over 3,500 years ago in the Middle East. Today its practitioners, Jews, are largely concentrated in Israel and the United States, with smaller populations in other countries around the world.

Kristallnacht: also known as "The Night of Broken Glass," *Kristallnacht* was a pogrom (violent riot) against Jews living across Germany in November 1938. Thousands of Jews were beaten by gangs and their property was attacked.

Liberalism: a political movement associated with maximizing the freedom of the individual, free trade, and moderate, continuous reform.

Marxism: a political ideology influenced by the writings and methods of German philosopher Karl Marx (1818–83). Marxists believe that capitalism will be destroyed by its own contradictions and replaced with a more egalitarian communist system.

Mein Kampf: an autobiography written by Adolf Hitler in the 1920s, in which he expressed his political ideas. The title means "my struggle."

Nazi: a shortened version of the National Socialist party name. The Nazis ruled Germany between 1933 and 1945 and were led by Adolf Hitler.

New Republic: the leading American liberal political magazine, first published in 1914.

Nuremberg Trials: held by the Allies in Nuremberg after the end of the World War II, these trials charged the Nazi political and administrative elite with war crimes.

Old Testament: the first part of the Christian Bible, which features texts written over a number of centuries. These writings are also sacred to the Jewish faith (and are known by Jews as the Tanakh).

Ottoman Empire: an empire with Istanbul at its heart, which expanded to include much of Anatolia, the Levant, and the Balkans. It collapsed in 1918 after military defeat in World War I.

Reformation: refers to the split in European Christianity in the sixteenth century, which began with a critique of the authority of the Pope over the Church and led to the formation of the Protestant churches.

Reserve Police Battalion 101: a police unit made up of men who were predominantly middle-aged and working–class Germans— "ordinary men"—who were either too old for the army or who volunteered to gain exemption from military draft. Both Goldhagen and historian Christopher Browning wrote about this Bavarian unit.

Scientific racism: a view that flourished in the nineteenth and twentieth centuries, based on new research into heredity and racial difference. Racist theorists and doctors tried to provide biological explanations for the diversity of human cultures and societies, and often proposed one race as superior to another. Such science was closely linked to eugenics, which sought to control the reproductive behavior of citizens in order to protect the perceived health of a nation.

Sonderweg: the German term for "special path." It was first used by late nineteenth-century German conservatives, before being adopted by historians such as Hans-Ulrich Wehler to describe the origins of Germany's turn to militarism and violence in the twentieth century.

Soviet Union: a communist state that lasted from 1922 to 1991 based on the principles of Marxist-Leninism. It encompassed Russia and surrounding states in Eastern Europe and Central Asia.

The SS: the short term for Schutzstaffel (Protection Squadron) that was the Nazis' elite paramilitary organization. Led by Heinrich Himmler, it was responsible for many of the worst atrocities of World War II, including the Holocaust.

The Third Reich: the common English term for the period of Nazi Party rule in Germany, which lasted from 1933 to 1945. During this period, both Germany and the Nazi Party were led by Adolf Hitler.

Time **magazine:** an American weekly news magazine founded in 1923 and published in New York City. It has a readership of 25 million and the world's largest circulation for a weekly news magazine.

World War I (1914–18): an international conflict centered in Europe and involving the major economic world powers of the day.

World War II (1939–45): a global conflict fought between the Axis Powers (Germany, Italy, and Japan) and the victorious Allied Powers (the United Kingdom and its colonies, the Soviet Union, and the United States).

Zionism: the foundational ideology of the state of Israel. Formulated by Theodor Herzl at the dawn of the twentieth century, it defended the project of Jewish resettlement in the ancestral lands of the Old Testament, in the territory of Palestine.

PEOPLE MENTIONED IN THE TEXT

Omer Bartov (b. 1953) is an Israeli-born historian who is professor of European history at Brown University. He has written widely on Jewish life in Galicia and the atrocities carried out by the regular German army, the Wehrmacht.

Yehuda Bauer (b. 1926) is a Czech-born Israeli historian of the Holocaust, based at the University of Jerusalem. Bauer was a key proponent of the intentionalist school of Holocaust interpretation.

Ruth Bettina Birn is a Canadian historian who has worked on the history of war crimes in association with the Canadian Justice Department. She has been among the fiercest critics of Goldhagen.

Y. Michal Bodemann is a professor of sociology at the University of Toronto, who has worked extensively on German Jews and the "ideological labor" performed by minority groups in social discourse.

Christopher Browning (b. 1944) completed his doctorate in 1975 and taught history at Pacific Lutheran University in Washington from 1974 to 1999, before moving to the University of North Carolina, where he currently teaches.

Jane Caplan is visiting professor at Birkbeck College, University of London, and is a historian of women's experience, administrative practices, and the concentration camps in Nazi Germany.

Alon Confino is an Israeli-born professor of history at Corcoran University, who has published widely on memory cultures in Germany, issues of historical method, and the cultural and ideological roots of anti-Semitism—what he calls the fantasy of a "world without Jews."

István Deák (b. 1926) is a Hungarian historian who taught for many years at Columbia and Stanford Universities, and has published widely on collaboration and resistance in Hitler's Europe.

Geoff Eley (b. 1949) is professor of history at the University of Michigan, and one of the foremost left-wing historians of the German Second Empire. In 2005's *The Crooked Line* he traced the changing fortunes of social history.

Richard Evans (b. 1947) is a British historian of modern Germany. He is most famous for a trilogy of books published between 2003 and 2008 known as *The Third Reich Trilogy*. He is currently Regius Professor of Modern History at Cambridge University.

Norman Finkelstein (b. 1953) is an American political scientist and author. Also the son of a Holocaust survivor, he has written highly controversial works on the Israel–Palestine conflict and the creation of a "Holocaust Industry."

Saul Friedländer (b. 1932) is a Czech-born Israeli historian, now based in UCLA in California. Friedländer's dense, sensitive books on the Holocaust—such as *The Years of Extermination*—are widely hailed as masterful interpretations.

Robert Gellately (b. 1943) is a Canadian-born historian who is a professor at Florida University and a specialist on European history during World War II and the Cold War.

Jan Gross (b. 1943) is professor of history and sociology at Princeton University and author of acclaimed and controversial books about the Polish role in anti-Semitic violence during and after World War II.

Heinrich Himmler (1900–45) was a leading member of the Nazi party and head of the SS. He played a decisive role in ordering the extermination of Jews in Eastern Europe and pushing ahead with the Final Solution.

Adolf Hitler (1889–45) was the Austrian-born leader of the Nazi Party who became Chancellor of Germany in 1933. Dismantling all opposition, Hitler set himself up as a dictator. His expansionist policies led to World War II, which saw the total defeat and destruction of his regime in 1945.

Eberhard Jäckel (b. 1929) is a German historian who taught for many years at Stuttgart University and published widely on Hitler's place in modern history.

Ian Kershaw (b. 1943) is a British historian of twentieth-century Germany. He has written extensively about the Third Reich and the Holocaust, and is best known for his two-part biography of Hitler, published in 1998 and 2000.

Walter Laqueur (b. 1921) is an American professor and historian who has written a large number of works about many topics, including Israeli history and the Holocaust.

Peter Longerich (b. 1955) is a German professor and historian who has worked at the Fritz Bauer Institute in Frankfurt and now at Royal Holloway College in London. He is a leading expert in the study of the Holocaust, and has written an acclaimed biography of Heinrich Himmler.

Martin Luther (1483–1546) was a German monk who launched the Protestant Reformation. Although Luther offered a radical critique of the Church, it has been argued that he retained, and even strengthened, the Church's tradition of anti-Semitism.

Mark Mazower (b. 1958) is a British historian of modern Europe. He has written extensively about the Third Reich, most recently in 2008's *Hitler's Empire: Nazi Rule in Occupied Europe.* He teaches at Columbia University.

Arno J. Mayer (b. 1926) is a professor at Princeton University, and has published widely on nineteenth-century Europe, the Holocaust, and revolutionary violence.

Herman Melville (1819–91) was an American novelist and author of *Moby Dick*, a novel cited by Goldhagen because he saw a parallel between the lead character, Captain Ahab, and his delusional hunt for his enemy, the whale, and the irrational German quest to destroy the Jews.

Hans Mommsen (b. 1930) is a left-wing German historian of the Nazi period and the German working class. He was the foremost exponent of a functionalist interpretation of Nazi racial policy.

A. D. Moses (b. 1967) is an Australian historian of the Holocaust and genocide generally. He is currently the chair in Global and Colonial History at the European University Institute in Florence, Italy.

George Mosse (1918–99) was a German-born American historian, famed for his works on nationalism, masculinity, mass politics, and the political origins of Nazism.

Ernst Nolte (b. 1923) is professor emeritus at the Free University of Berlin. He is famed for his comparative work on communism and fascism, which helped trigger the *Historikerstreit* in the 1980s.

Timothy Snyder (b. 1969) is an American historian and the author of *Bloodlands: Europe Between Hitler and Stalin* (2010). He teaches at Yale University.

Albert Speer (1905–81) was an architect and confidant of Hitler, who became minister of armaments during World War II. He was spared at the Nuremberg trials and instead sentenced to detention at Spandau. The extent to which Speer was genuinely repentant about his Nazi past has been hotly debated.

Fritz Stern (b. 1926) was a German-born American historian of historiography and German politics, who became professor emeritus at Columbia University, New York. Among his most famous works was *The Politics of Cultural Despair*. He was very critical of Goldhagen, calling him Germanophobic.

Dan Stone is a professor at Royal Holloway College, University of London, who has written widely on the historiography of the Holocaust, the liberation of the camps, and the emergence of a new Europe after 1945.

Enzo Traverso (b. 1957) is an Italian historian. He has written extensively about the Holocaust, most notably in *The Origins of Nazi Violence*. He teaches at Cornell University.

Shulamit Volkov (b. 1942) is a professor at Tel Aviv University and a historian of labor relations and anti-Semitism in nineteenth-century Germany.

Hans-Ulrich Wehler (1931–2014) was a pioneering German social historian, a leader of the Bielefeld School, famed for his work on imperial Germany.

Elie Wiesel (b. 1928) was born in Romania and survived both Auschwitz and Buchenwald concentration camps. Following World War II, Wiesel published a memoir of his experiences in the camps, *Night*, which has gone on to sell over 10 million copies worldwide. In 1986, he was awarded the Nobel Peace Prize for his activism against violence and racism.

WORKS CITED

WORKS CITED

Aschheim, Steven E. "Archetypes and the German Jewish Dialogue: Reflections Occasioned by the Goldhagen Affair." *German History* 15, no. 2 (1997): 240–50.

Barnett, Victoria. *For the Soul of the People: Protestant Protest Against Hitler*. New York: Oxford University Press, 1992.

Bartov, Omer. "Ordinary Monsters." *The New Republic*, April 29, 1996, 32–8.

"Reception and Perception: Goldhagen's Holocaust and the World." In *The "Goldhagen Effect": History, Memory, Nazism—Facing the German Past*, edited by Geoff Eley, 33–89. Ann Arbor: University of Michigan Press, 2000.

Bauer, Yehuda. *A History of the Holocaust*. New York: F. Watts, 1982.

Rethinking the Holocaust. New Haven, CT: Yale University Press, 2000.

Bauman, Zygmunt. *Modernity and the Holocaust*. Cambridge: Polity, 1989.

Bodemann, Y. Michal. "Die Bösen und die ganz normalen Guten." *Die Tageszeitung*, August 7, 1996.

Browning, Christopher. *Ordinary Men: Reserve Police Battalion 101 and the Final Solution in Poland*. New York: HarperCollins, 1992.

Caplan, Jane. "Reflections on the Reception of Goldhagen in the United States." In *The "Goldhagen Effect": History, Memory, Nazism—Facing the German Past*, edited by Geoff Eley, 151–63. Ann Arbor: University of Michigan Press, 2000.

Cesarini, David. "The Aftermath of the Holocaust." In *Encyclopedia of the Holocaust*, edited by Shmuel Spector and Robert Rozett, 85–100. New York and London: Routledge, 2013.

Clendinnean, Inga. "The Men in the Green Tunics." In *Reading the Holocaust*, 133–55. Cambridge: Cambridge University Press, 1998.

Confino, Alon. "Fantasies about the Jews: Cultural Reflections on the

Holocaust." *History & Memory* 17, nos. 1–2 (2005): 296–322.

Foundational Pasts: The Holocaust as Historical Understanding. Cambridge: Cambridge University Press, 2013.

A World Without Jews: The Nazi Imagination from Persecution to Genocide. New Haven, London: Yale University Press, 2014.

Cornwell, John. *Hitler's Pope: The Secret History of Pius XII*. London,

New York: Penguin, 1999.

Eley, Geoff. "Ordinary Germans, Nazis, and Judeocide." In *The "Goldhagen Effect": History, Memory, Nazism—Facing the German Past*, edited by Geoff Eley, 1–33. Ann Arbor: University of Michigan Press, 2000.

Evans, Richard. *The Coming of the Third Reich*. London: Penguin, 2004.

"In Pursuit of the Untertanengeist: Crime, Law and Social Order in German History." In *Rethinking German History: Nineteenth-Century Germany and the Origins of the Third Reich*, 156–87. London: Allen & Unwin, 1987.

The Third Reich at War. London: Penguin, 2009.

"Written into History." *London Review of Books* 37, no. 2 (January 22, 2015): 17–19.

Finkelstein, Norman G. "Daniel Jonah Goldhagen's 'Crazy' Thesis: A Critique of Hitler's Willing Executioners." *New Left Review* 1, no. 224 (July–August 1997): 39–87.

Finkelstein, Norman G., and Ruth Bettina Birn. *A Nation on Trial: The Goldhagen Thesis and Historical Truth*. New York: Metropolitan Books, 1998.

Friedländer, Saul. *Probing the Limits of Representation: Nazism and the "Final Solution."* Cambridge MA: Harvard University Press, 1992.

Gellateley, Robert. "Review: *Hitler's Willing Executioners: Ordinary Germans and the Holocaust*." *Journal of Modern History* 69, no. 1 (1997): 187–91.

Goldhagen, Daniel Jonah. *The Devil That Never Dies: The Rise and Threat of Global Antisemitism*. London: Little, Brown, 2013.

"The Evil of Banality." *New Republic*, July 13/20, 1992, 49–52.

"False Witness." *New Republic*, April 17, 1989, 39–42.

"The Fictions of Ruth Bettina Birn." *German Politics and Society* 15, no.3 (1997): 119–65.

Hitler's Willing Executioners: Ordinary Germans and the Holocaust. New York: Vintage Books, 1997.

"How Could They Have Done It?" *Harvard University Gazette*, June 6, 1996. Accessed April 22, 2015. http://news.harvard.edu/gazette/1996/06.06/HowCouldTheyHav.html.

"Mass Slaughter is a Systemic Problem of the Modern World." *Der Spiegel*, October 8, 2009.

A Moral Reckoning: The Role of the Catholic Church in the Holocaust and Its Unfulfilled Duty of Repair. New York: Alfred A. Knopf, 2002.

"Motives, Causes, and Alibis.' *New Republic*, December 23, 1996, 37–45.

Worse Than War: Genocide, Eliminationism, and the Ongoing Assault on Humanity. New York: Public Affairs, 2009.

Goldhagen, Erich. "Albert Speer, Himmler and the Secrecy of the Final Solution." *Midstream* (October 1971): 43–50.

Gross, Jan. *Fear: Anti-Semitism in Poland after Auschwitz. An Essay in Historical Interpretation*. Princeton: Princeton University Press, 2006.

Neighbours: The Destruction of the Jewish Community in Jedwabne, Poland. Princeton: Princeton University Press, 2001.

Herf, Jeffrey. *Divided Memory: Nazi Past in the Two Germanys*. Cambridge

MA: Harvard University Press, 1997.

Hull, Isabel. *Absolute Destruction: Military Culture and the Practices of War in Imperial Germany*. Ithaca: Cornell University Press, 2006.

Jäckel, Eberhard. "Einfach ein schlechtes Buch." *Die Zeit*, May 17, 1996, 39.

Jäckel, Eberhard, and Jürgen Rohwer, eds. *Der Mord an den Juden im Zweiten Weltkrieg: Entschlußbildung und Verwirklichung*. Stuttgart: Deutsche Verlag-Anstalt, 1985.

Jenkins, Philip. *The New Anti-Catholicism: The Last Acceptable Prejudice*. Oxford: Oxford University Press, 2003.

Johnson, Eric. *Nazi Terror: The Gestapo, Jews and Ordinary Germans*. New York: Basic Books, 2000.

Kelman, Herbert C., and V. Lee Hamilton. *Crimes of Obedience: Toward a Social Psychology of Authority and Responsibility*. New Haven, CT: Yale University Press, 1989.

Kershaw, Ian. *Hitler: A Biography*. New York: W.W. Norton, 2008.

Langbehn, Volker, and Mohammad Salama, eds. *German Colonialism: Race, the Holocaust and Postwar Germany*. New York: Columbia University Press, 2013.

Lowe, Keith. *Savage Continent: Europe in the Aftermath of World War*.

London, New York: Viking, 2012.

Mazower, Mark. *Dark Continent: Europe's Twentieth Century*. New York: Knopf, 1999.

Hitler's Empire: Nazi Rule in Occupied Europe. London: Penguin, 2008.

Midlarsky, Manus. *The Killing Trap: Genocide in the Twentieth Century*. Cambridge: Cambridge University Press, 2005.

Mommsen, Hans. "Die dünne Patina der Zivilisation." *Die Zeit*, August 30, 1996, 14.

"Cumulative Radicalisation and Progressive Self-Destruction as Structural Determinants of the Nazi Dictatorship." In *Stalinism and Nazism: Dictatorships in Comparison*, edited by Ian Kershaw and Moshe Lewin, 75–87. Cambridge: Cambridge University Press, 1997.

Moses, A.D. "Structure and Agency in the Holocaust: Daniel J. Goldhagen and His Critics." *History and Theory* 37, no. 2 (1998): 194–219.

Mosse, George. *The Crisis of German Ideology: Intellectual Origins of the Third Reich*. New York: Schocken Books, 1981.

Neumann, Klaus. *Shifting Memories: The Nazi Past in the New Germany*. Michigan: University of Michigan Press, 2000.

Nolte, Ernst. "Die Vergangenheit, die nicht vergehen will." *Frankfurter Allgemeine Zeitung*, June 6, 1986.

Das Vergehen der Vergangenheit: Antwort an meine Kritiker in sogenannten Historikerstreit. Berlin: Ullstein, 1987.

North, David. *Anti-Semitism, Fascism and the Holocaust: A Critical Review of Daniel Goldhagen's* Hitler's Willing Executioners. Michigan: Labor Publications, 1996.

Olusoga, David, and Casper Erichsen. *The Kaiser's Holocaust: Germany's Forgotten Genocide and the Colonial Roots of Nazism*. London: Faber and Faber, 2011.

Rieger, Bernard. "'Daniel in the Lion's Den?' The German Debate about Goldhagen's *Hitler's Willing Executioners*." *History Workshop Journal* 43 (1997): 226–33.

Röhl, John. "Ordinary Germans as Hitler's Willing Executioners? The Goldhagen Controversy." In *Historical Controversies and Historians*, edited by William Lamont, 15–23. London: UCL Press, 1998.

Rosenberg, Hans. *Bureaucracy, Aristocracy, and Autocracy: The Prussian Experience, 1600–1815*. Boston, MA: Beacon Press, 1968.

Ruder, Debra Bradley. "Goldhagen Wins German Prize for Holocaust Book." *Harvard University Gazette*, January 9, 1997. Accessed April 22, 2015. http://www.news.harvard.edu/gazette/1997/01.09/GoldhagenWinsGe.html.

Schoenbaum, David. "Ordinary People?" *National Review* 48 (July 1, 1996): 54–55.

Shandley, Robert R., ed. *Unwilling Germans?: The Goldhagen Debate*. Minneapolis: University of Minnesota Press, 1998.

Smith, Dinita. "Challenging a View of the Holocaust." *New York Times*, April 1, 1996. Accessed April 22, 2015. http://www.nytimes.com/1996/04/01/books/challenging-a-view-of-the-holocaust.html.

Snyder, Timothy. *Bloodlands: Europe Between Hitler and Stalin*. New York: Basic Books, 2010.

"Holocaust: The Ignored Reality." *New York Review of Books*, July 16, 2009.

"A New Approach to the Holocaust." *New York Review of Books*, June 23, 2011.

Stern, Fritz. *The Politics of Cultural Despair: A Study in the Rise of the Germanic Ideology*. Berkeley: University of California Press, 1974.

Stone, Dan. "Holocaust Historiography and Cultural History." In *The Holocaust and Historical Methodology*, 52–68. New York: Bergahan, 2012.

Traub, James. "Patterns of Genocide." *New York Times*, October 15, 2009. Accessed April 22, 2015. http://www.nytimes.com/2009/10/18/books/review/Traub-t.html.

Traverso, Enzo. *The Origins of Nazi Violence*. Translated by Janet Lloyd. New York: New Press, 2003.

Wehler, Hans-Ulrich. "The Goldhagen Controversy: Agonizing Problems, Scholarly Failure and the Political Dimension." *German History* 15, no. 1 (1997): 80–91.

"Wie ein Stachel im Fleisch." *Die Zeit*, May 24, 1996, 40.

Zahn, Gordon. *German Catholics and Hitler's Wars: A Study in Social Control*. Indiana: Notre Dame University Press, 1988.

Zangwill, Nick. "Perpetrator Motivation: Some Reflections on the Goldhagen/Browning Debate." In *Moral Philosophy and the Holocaust*, edited by Eve Garrard and Geoffrey Scarre, 89–102. Basingstoke: Ashgate, 2003.

THE MACAT LIBRARY
BY DISCIPLINE

AFRICANA STUDIES

Chinua Achebe's *An Image of Africa: Racism in Conrad's Heart of Darkness*
W. E. B. Du Bois's *The Souls of Black Folk*
Zora Neale Huston's *Characteristics of Negro Expression*
Martin Luther King Jr's *Why We Can't Wait*
Toni Morrison's *Playing in the Dark: Whiteness in the American Literary Imagination*

ANTHROPOLOGY

Arjun Appadurai's *Modernity at Large: Cultural Dimensions of Globalisation*
Philippe Ariès's *Centuries of Childhood*
Franz Boas's *Race, Language and Culture*
Kim Chan & Renée Mauborgne's *Blue Ocean Strategy*
Jared Diamond's *Guns, Germs & Steel: the Fate of Human Societies*
Jared Diamond's *Collapse: How Societies Choose to Fail or Survive*
E. E. Evans-Pritchard's *Witchcraft, Oracles and Magic Among the Azande*
James Ferguson's *The Anti-Politics Machine*
Clifford Geertz's *The Interpretation of Cultures*
David Graeber's *Debt: the First 5000 Years*
Karen Ho's *Liquidated: An Ethnography of Wall Street*
Geert Hofstede's *Culture's Consequences: Comparing Values, Behaviors, Institutes and Organizations across Nations*
Claude Lévi-Strauss's *Structural Anthropology*
Jay Macleod's *Ain't No Makin' It: Aspirations and Attainment in a Low-Income Neighborhood*
Saba Mahmood's *The Politics of Piety: The Islamic Revival and the Feminist Subject*
Marcel Mauss's *The Gift*

BUSINESS

Jean Lave & Etienne Wenger's *Situated Learning*
Theodore Levitt's *Marketing Myopia*
Burton G. Malkiel's *A Random Walk Down Wall Street*
Douglas McGregor's *The Human Side of Enterprise*
Michael Porter's *Competitive Strategy: Creating and Sustaining Superior Performance*
John Kotter's *Leading Change*
C. K. Prahalad & Gary Hamel's *The Core Competence of the Corporation*

CRIMINOLOGY

Michelle Alexander's *The New Jim Crow: Mass Incarceration in the Age of Colorblindness*
Michael R. Gottfredson & Travis Hirschi's *A General Theory of Crime*
Richard Herrnstein & Charles A. Murray's *The Bell Curve: Intelligence and Class Structure in American Life*
Elizabeth Loftus's *Eyewitness Testimony*
Jay Macleod's *Ain't No Makin' It: Aspirations and Attainment in a Low-Income Neighborhood*
Philip Zimbardo's *The Lucifer Effect*

ECONOMICS

Janet Abu-Lughod's *Before European Hegemony*
Ha-Joon Chang's *Kicking Away the Ladder*
David Brion Davis's *The Problem of Slavery in the Age of Revolution*
Milton Friedman's *The Role of Monetary Policy*
Milton Friedman's *Capitalism and Freedom*
David Graeber's *Debt: the First 5000 Years*
Friedrich Hayek's *The Road to Serfdom*
Karen Ho's *Liquidated: An Ethnography of Wall Street*

John Maynard Keynes's *The General Theory of Employment, Interest and Money*
Charles P. Kindleberger's *Manias, Panics and Crashes*
Robert Lucas's *Why Doesn't Capital Flow from Rich to Poor Countries?*
Burton G. Malkiel's *A Random Walk Down Wall Street*
Thomas Robert Malthus's *An Essay on the Principle of Population*
Karl Marx's *Capital*
Thomas Piketty's *Capital in the Twenty-First Century*
Amartya Sen's *Development as Freedom*
Adam Smith's *The Wealth of Nations*
Nassim Nicholas Taleb's *The Black Swan: The Impact of the Highly Improbable*
Amos Tversky's & Daniel Kahneman's *Judgment under Uncertainty: Heuristics and Biases*
Mahbub Ul Haq's *Reflections on Human Development*
Max Weber's *The Protestant Ethic and the Spirit of Capitalism*

FEMINISM AND GENDER STUDIES

Judith Butler's *Gender Trouble*
Simone De Beauvoir's *The Second Sex*
Michel Foucault's *History of Sexuality*
Betty Friedan's *The Feminine Mystique*
Saba Mahmood's *The Politics of Piety: The Islamic Revival and the Feminist Subject*
Joan Wallach Scott's *Gender and the Politics of History*
Mary Wollstonecraft's *A Vindication of the Rights of Woman*
Virginia Woolf's *A Room of One's Own*

GEOGRAPHY

The Brundtland Report's *Our Common Future*
Rachel Carson's *Silent Spring*
Charles Darwin's *On the Origin of Species*
James Ferguson's *The Anti-Politics Machine*
Jane Jacobs's *The Death and Life of Great American Cities*
James Lovelock's *Gaia: A New Look at Life on Earth*
Amartya Sen's *Development as Freedom*
Mathis Wackernagel & William Rees's *Our Ecological Footprint*

HISTORY

Janet Abu-Lughod's *Before European Hegemony*
Benedict Anderson's *Imagined Communities*
Bernard Bailyn's *The Ideological Origins of the American Revolution*
Hanna Batatu's *The Old Social Classes And The Revolutionary Movements Of Iraq*
Christopher Browning's *Ordinary Men: Reserve Police Batallion 101 and the Final Solution in Poland*
Edmund Burke's *Reflections on the Revolution in France*
William Cronon's *Nature's Metropolis: Chicago And The Great West*
Alfred W. Crosby's *The Columbian Exchange*
Hamid Dabashi's *Iran: A People Interrupted*
David Brion Davis's *The Problem of Slavery in the Age of Revolution*
Nathalie Zemon Davis's *The Return of Martin Guerre*
Jared Diamond's *Guns, Germs & Steel: the Fate of Human Societies*
Frank Dikotter's *Mao's Great Famine*
John W Dower's *War Without Mercy: Race And Power In The Pacific War*
W. E. B. Du Bois's *The Souls of Black Folk*
Richard J. Evans's *In Defence of History*
Lucien Febvre's *The Problem of Unbelief in the 16th Century*
Sheila Fitzpatrick's *Everyday Stalinism*

The Macat Library By Discipline

Eric Foner's *Reconstruction: America's Unfinished Revolution, 1863-1877*
Michel Foucault's *Discipline and Punish*
Michel Foucault's *History of Sexuality*
Francis Fukuyama's *The End of History and the Last Man*
John Lewis Gaddis's *We Now Know: Rethinking Cold War History*
Ernest Gellner's *Nations and Nationalism*
Eugene Genovese's *Roll, Jordan, Roll: The World the Slaves Made*
Carlo Ginzburg's *The Night Battles*
Daniel Goldhagen's *Hitler's Willing Executioners*
Jack Goldstone's *Revolution and Rebellion in the Early Modern World*
Antonio Gramsci's *The Prison Notebooks*
Alexander Hamilton, John Jay & James Madison's *The Federalist Papers*
Christopher Hill's *The World Turned Upside Down*
Carole Hillenbrand's *The Crusades: Islamic Perspectives*
Thomas Hobbes's *Leviathan*
Eric Hobsbawm's *The Age Of Revolution*
John A. Hobson's *Imperialism: A Study*
Albert Hourani's *History of the Arab Peoples*
Samuel P. Huntington's *The Clash of Civilizations and the Remaking of World Order*
C. L. R. James's *The Black Jacobins*
Tony Judt's *Postwar: A History of Europe Since 1945*
Ernst Kantorowicz's *The King's Two Bodies: A Study in Medieval Political Theology*
Paul Kennedy's *The Rise and Fall of the Great Powers*
Ian Kershaw's *The "Hitler Myth": Image and Reality in the Third Reich*
John Maynard Keynes's *The General Theory of Employment, Interest and Money*
Charles P. Kindleberger's *Manias, Panics and Crashes*
Martin Luther King Jr's *Why We Can't Wait*
Henry Kissinger's *World Order: Reflections on the Character of Nations and the Course of History*
Thomas Kuhn's *The Structure of Scientific Revolutions*
Georges Lefebvre's *The Coming of the French Revolution*
John Locke's *Two Treatises of Government*
Niccolò Machiavelli's *The Prince*
Thomas Robert Malthus's *An Essay on the Principle of Population*
Mahmood Mamdani's *Citizen and Subject: Contemporary Africa And The Legacy Of Late Colonialism*
Karl Marx's *Capital*
Stanley Milgram's *Obedience to Authority*
John Stuart Mill's *On Liberty*
Thomas Paine's *Common Sense*
Thomas Paine's *Rights of Man*
Geoffrey Parker's *Global Crisis: War, Climate Change and Catastrophe in the Seventeenth Century*
Jonathan Riley-Smith's *The First Crusade and the Idea of Crusading*
Jean-Jacques Rousseau's *The Social Contract*
Joan Wallach Scott's *Gender and the Politics of History*
Theda Skocpol's *States and Social Revolutions*
Adam Smith's *The Wealth of Nations*
Timothy Snyder's *Bloodlands: Europe Between Hitler and Stalin*
Sun Tzu's *The Art of War*
Keith Thomas's *Religion and the Decline of Magic*
Thucydides's *The History of the Peloponnesian War*
Frederick Jackson Turner's *The Significance of the Frontier in American History*
Odd Arne Westad's *The Global Cold War: Third World Interventions And The Making Of Our Times*

LITERATURE

Chinua Achebe's *An Image of Africa: Racism in Conrad's Heart of Darkness*
Roland Barthes's *Mythologies*
Homi K. Bhabha's *The Location of Culture*
Judith Butler's *Gender Trouble*
Simone De Beauvoir's *The Second Sex*
Ferdinand De Saussure's *Course in General Linguistics*
T. S. Eliot's *The Sacred Wood: Essays on Poetry and Criticism*
Zora Neale Huston's *Characteristics of Negro Expression*
Toni Morrison's *Playing in the Dark: Whiteness in the American Literary Imagination*
Edward Said's *Orientalism*
Gayatri Chakravorty Spivak's *Can the Subaltern Speak?*
Mary Wollstonecraft's *A Vindication of the Rights of Women*
Virginia Woolf's *A Room of One's Own*

PHILOSOPHY

Elizabeth Anscombe's *Modern Moral Philosophy*
Hannah Arendt's *The Human Condition*
Aristotle's *Metaphysics*
Aristotle's *Nicomachean Ethics*
Edmund Gettier's *Is Justified True Belief Knowledge?*
Georg Wilhelm Friedrich Hegel's *Phenomenology of Spirit*
David Hume's *Dialogues Concerning Natural Religion*
David Hume's *The Enquiry for Human Understanding*
Immanuel Kant's *Religion within the Boundaries of Mere Reason*
Immanuel Kant's *Critique of Pure Reason*
Søren Kierkegaard's *The Sickness Unto Death*
Søren Kierkegaard's *Fear and Trembling*
C. S. Lewis's *The Abolition of Man*
Alasdair MacIntyre's *After Virtue*
Marcus Aurelius's *Meditations*
Friedrich Nietzsche's *On the Genealogy of Morality*
Friedrich Nietzsche's *Beyond Good and Evil*
Plato's *Republic*
Plato's *Symposium*
Jean-Jacques Rousseau's *The Social Contract*
Gilbert Ryle's *The Concept of Mind*
Baruch Spinoza's *Ethics*
Sun Tzu's *The Art of War*
Ludwig Wittgenstein's *Philosophical Investigations*

POLITICS

Benedict Anderson's *Imagined Communities*
Aristotle's *Politics*
Bernard Bailyn's *The Ideological Origins of the American Revolution*
Edmund Burke's *Reflections on the Revolution in France*
John C. Calhoun's *A Disquisition on Government*
Ha-Joon Chang's *Kicking Away the Ladder*
Hamid Dabashi's *Iran: A People Interrupted*
Hamid Dabashi's *Theology of Discontent: The Ideological Foundation of the Islamic Revolution in Iran*
Robert Dahl's *Democracy and its Critics*
Robert Dahl's *Who Governs?*
David Brion Davis's *The Problem of Slavery in the Age of Revolution*

The Macat Library By Discipline

Alexis De Tocqueville's *Democracy in America*
James Ferguson's *The Anti-Politics Machine*
Frank Dikotter's *Mao's Great Famine*
Sheila Fitzpatrick's *Everyday Stalinism*
Eric Foner's *Reconstruction: America's Unfinished Revolution, 1863-1877*
Milton Friedman's *Capitalism and Freedom*
Francis Fukuyama's *The End of History and the Last Man*
John Lewis Gaddis's *We Now Know: Rethinking Cold War History*
Ernest Gellner's *Nations and Nationalism*
David Graeber's *Debt: the First 5000 Years*
Antonio Gramsci's *The Prison Notebooks*
Alexander Hamilton, John Jay & James Madison's *The Federalist Papers*
Friedrich Hayek's *The Road to Serfdom*
Christopher Hill's *The World Turned Upside Down*
Thomas Hobbes's *Leviathan*
John A. Hobson's *Imperialism: A Study*
Samuel P. Huntington's *The Clash of Civilizations and the Remaking of World Order*
Tony Judt's *Postwar: A History of Europe Since 1945*
David C. Kang's *China Rising: Peace, Power and Order in East Asia*
Paul Kennedy's *The Rise and Fall of Great Powers*
Robert Keohane's *After Hegemony*
Martin Luther King Jr.'s *Why We Can't Wait*
Henry Kissinger's *World Order: Reflections on the Character of Nations and the Course of History*
John Locke's *Two Treatises of Government*
Niccolò Machiavelli's *The Prince*
Thomas Robert Malthus's *An Essay on the Principle of Population*
Mahmood Mamdani's *Citizen and Subject: Contemporary Africa And The Legacy Of*
Late Colonialism
Karl Marx's *Capital*
John Stuart Mill's *On Liberty*
John Stuart Mill's *Utilitarianism*
Hans Morgenthau's *Politics Among Nations*
Thomas Paine's *Common Sense*
Thomas Paine's *Rights of Man*
Thomas Piketty's *Capital in the Twenty-First Century*
Robert D. Putman's *Bowling Alone*
John Rawls's *Theory of Justice*
Jean-Jacques Rousseau's *The Social Contract*
Theda Skocpol's *States and Social Revolutions*
Adam Smith's *The Wealth of Nations*
Sun Tzu's *The Art of War*
Henry David Thoreau's *Civil Disobedience*
Thucydides's *The History of the Peloponnesian War*
Kenneth Waltz's *Theory of International Politics*
Max Weber's *Politics as a Vocation*
Odd Arne Westad's *The Global Cold War: Third World Interventions And The Making Of Our Times*

POSTCOLONIAL STUDIES

Roland Barthes's *Mythologies*
Frantz Fanon's *Black Skin, White Masks*
Homi K. Bhabha's *The Location of Culture*
Gustavo Gutiérrez's *A Theology of Liberation*
Edward Said's *Orientalism*
Gayatri Chakravorty Spivak's *Can the Subaltern Speak?*

PSYCHOLOGY

Gordon Allport's *The Nature of Prejudice*
Alan Baddeley & Graham Hitch's *Aggression: A Social Learning Analysis*
Albert Bandura's *Aggression: A Social Learning Analysis*
Leon Festinger's *A Theory of Cognitive Dissonance*
Sigmund Freud's *The Interpretation of Dreams*
Betty Friedan's *The Feminine Mystique*
Michael R. Gottfredson & Travis Hirschi's *A General Theory of Crime*
Eric Hoffer's *The True Believer: Thoughts on the Nature of Mass Movements*
William James's *Principles of Psychology*
Elizabeth Loftus's *Eyewitness Testimony*
A. H. Maslow's *A Theory of Human Motivation*
Stanley Milgram's *Obedience to Authority*
Steven Pinker's *The Better Angels of Our Nature*
Oliver Sacks's *The Man Who Mistook His Wife For a Hat*
Richard Thaler & Cass Sunstein's *Nudge: Improving Decisions About Health, Wealth and Happiness*
Amos Tversky's *Judgment under Uncertainty: Heuristics and Biases*
Philip Zimbardo's *The Lucifer Effect*

SCIENCE

Rachel Carson's *Silent Spring*
William Cronon's *Nature's Metropolis: Chicago And The Great West*
Alfred W. Crosby's *The Columbian Exchange*
Charles Darwin's *On the Origin of Species*
Richard Dawkin's *The Selfish Gene*
Thomas Kuhn's *The Structure of Scientific Revolutions*
Geoffrey Parker's *Global Crisis: War, Climate Change and Catastrophe in the Seventeenth Century*
Mathis Wackernagel & William Rees's *Our Ecological Footprint*

SOCIOLOGY

Michelle Alexander's *The New Jim Crow: Mass Incarceration in the Age of Colorblindness*
Gordon Allport's *The Nature of Prejudice*
Albert Bandura's *Aggression: A Social Learning Analysis*
Hanna Batatu's *The Old Social Classes And The Revolutionary Movements Of Iraq*
Ha-Joon Chang's *Kicking Away the Ladder*
W. E. B. Du Bois's *The Souls of Black Folk*
Émile Durkheim's *On Suicide*
Frantz Fanon's *Black Skin, White Masks*
Frantz Fanon's *The Wretched of the Earth*
Eric Foner's *Reconstruction: America's Unfinished Revolution, 1863-1877*
Eugene Genovese's *Roll, Jordan, Roll: The World the Slaves Made*
Jack Goldstone's *Revolution and Rebellion in the Early Modern World*
Antonio Gramsci's *The Prison Notebooks*
Richard Herrnstein & Charles A Murray's *The Bell Curve: Intelligence and Class Structure in American Life*
Eric Hoffer's *The True Believer: Thoughts on the Nature of Mass Movements*
Jane Jacobs's *The Death and Life of Great American Cities*
Robert Lucas's *Why Doesn't Capital Flow from Rich to Poor Countries?*
Jay Macleod's *Ain't No Makin' It: Aspirations and Attainment in a Low Income Neighborhood*
Elaine May's *Homeward Bound: American Families in the Cold War Era*
Douglas McGregor's *The Human Side of Enterprise*
C. Wright Mills's *The Sociological Imagination*

The Macat Library By Discipline

Thomas Piketty's *Capital in the Twenty-First Century*
Robert D. Putman's *Bowling Alone*
David Riesman's *The Lonely Crowd: A Study of the Changing American Character*
Edward Said's *Orientalism*
Joan Wallach Scott's *Gender and the Politics of History*
Theda Skocpol's *States and Social Revolutions*
Max Weber's *The Protestant Ethic and the Spirit of Capitalism*

THEOLOGY

Augustine's *Confessions*
Benedict's *Rule of St Benedict*
Gustavo Gutiérrez's *A Theology of Liberation*
Carole Hillenbrand's *The Crusades: Islamic Perspectives*
David Hume's *Dialogues Concerning Natural Religion*
Immanuel Kant's *Religion within the Boundaries of Mere Reason*
Ernst Kantorowicz's *The King's Two Bodies: A Study in Medieval Political Theology*
Søren Kierkegaard's *The Sickness Unto Death*
C. S. Lewis's *The Abolition of Man*
Saba Mahmood's *The Politics of Piety: The Islamic Revival and the Feminist Subject*
Baruch Spinoza's *Ethics*
Keith Thomas's *Religion and the Decline of Magic*

COMING SOON

Chris Argyris's *The Individual and the Organisation*
Seyla Benhabib's *The Rights of Others*
Walter Benjamin's *The Work Of Art in the Age of Mechanical Reproduction*
John Berger's *Ways of Seeing*
Pierre Bourdieu's *Outline of a Theory of Practice*
Mary Douglas's *Purity and Danger*
Roland Dworkin's *Taking Rights Seriously*
James G. March's *Exploration and Exploitation in Organisational Learning*
Ikujiro Nonaka's *A Dynamic Theory of Organizational Knowledge Creation*
Griselda Pollock's *Vision and Difference*
Amartya Sen's *Inequality Re-Examined*
Susan Sontag's *On Photography*
Yasser Tabbaa's *The Transformation of Islamic Art*
Ludwig von Mises's *Theory of Money and Credit*

Macat Disciplines

Access the greatest ideas and thinkers across entire disciplines, including

FEMINISM, GENDER AND QUEER STUDIES

Simone De Beauvoir's
The Second Sex

Michel Foucault's
History of Sexuality

Betty Friedan's
The Feminine Mystique

Saba Mahmood's
*The Politics of Piety:
The Islamic Revival and
the Feminist Subject*

Joan Wallach Scott's
*Gender and the
Politics of History*

Mary Wollstonecraft's
*A Vindication of the
Rights of Woman*

Virginia Woolf's
A Room of One's Own

Judith Butler's
Gender Trouble

 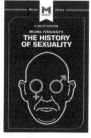  

Macat Disciplines

Access the greatest ideas and thinkers across entire disciplines, including

INEQUALITY

Ha-Joon Chang's, *Kicking Away the Ladder*

David Graeber's, *Debt: The First 5000 Years*

Robert E. Lucas's, *Why Doesn't Capital Flow from Rich To Poor Countries?*

Thomas Piketty's, *Capital in the Twenty-First Century*

Amartya Sen's, *Inequality Re-Examined*

Mahbub Ul Haq's, *Reflections on Human Development*

Macat Disciplines

*Access the greatest ideas and thinkers
across entire disciplines, including*

CRIMINOLOGY

Michelle Alexander's
*The New Jim Crow:
Mass Incarceration in the
Age of Colorblindness*

**Michael R. Gottfredson
& Travis Hirschi's**
A General Theory of Crime

Elizabeth Loftus's
Eyewitness Testimony

**Richard Herrnstein
& Charles A. Murray's**
*The Bell Curve: Intelligence and
Class Structure in American Life*

Jay Macleod's
*Ain't No Makin' It:
Aspirations and Attainment in a
Low-Income Neighborhood*

Philip Zimbardo's
The Lucifer Effect

Macat Disciplines

Access the greatest ideas and thinkers across entire disciplines, including

Postcolonial Studies

Roland Barthes's *Mythologies*
Frantz Fanon's *Black Skin, White Masks*
Homi K. Bhabha's *The Location of Culture*
Gustavo Gutiérrez's *A Theology of Liberation*
Edward Said's *Orientalism*
Gayatri Chakravorty Spivak's *Can the Subaltern Speak?*

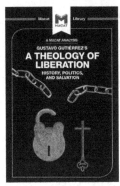

Macat analyses are available from all good bookshops and libraries.

Access hundreds of analyses through one, multimedia tool.

Join free for one month **library.macat.com**

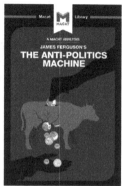

Macat Pairs

Analyse historical and modern issues from opposite sides of an argument. Pairs include:

HOW TO RUN AN ECONOMY

John Maynard Keynes's
The General Theory OF Employment, Interest and Money

Classical economics suggests that market economies are self-correcting in times of recession or depression, and tend toward full employment and output. But English economist John Maynard Keynes disagrees.

In his ground-breaking 1936 study *The General Theory*, Keynes argues that traditional economics has misunderstood the causes of unemployment. Employment is not determined by the price of labor; it is directly linked to demand. Keynes believes market economies are by nature unstable, and so require government intervention. Spurred on by the social catastrophe of the Great Depression of the 1930s, he sets out to revolutionize the way the world thinks

Milton Friedman's
The Role of Monetary Policy

Friedman's 1968 paper changed the course of economic theory. In just 17 pages, he demolished existing theory and outlined an effective alternate monetary policy designed to secure 'high employment, stable prices and rapid growth.'

Friedman demonstrated that monetary policy plays a vital role in broader economic stability and argued that economists got their monetary policy wrong in the 1950s and 1960s by misunderstanding the relationship between inflation and unemployment. Previous generations of economists had believed that governments could permanently decrease unemployment by permitting inflation—and vice versa. Friedman's most original contribution was to show that this supposed trade-off is an illusion that only works in the short term.

Macat analyses are available from all good bookshops and libraries.

Access hundreds of analyses through one, multimedia tool.
Join free for one month **library.macat.com**

Macat Disciplines

Access the greatest ideas and thinkers across entire disciplines, including

THE FUTURE OF DEMOCRACY

Robert A. Dahl's, *Democracy and Its Critics*
Robert A. Dahl's, *Who Governs?*
Alexis De Toqueville's, *Democracy in America*
Niccolò Machiavelli's, *The Prince*
John Stuart Mill's, *On Liberty*
Robert D. Putnam's, *Bowling Alone*
Jean-Jacques Rousseau's, *The Social Contract*
Henry David Thoreau's, *Civil Disobedience*

Printed in the United States
by Baker & Taylor Publisher Services